**Free To Be You**
By Larry Chkoreff
Version 6.1 May 2016
Original 2008
ISBN – 978-0-9823060-1-7
*Free To Be You* is published by, and is a discipleship curriculum of
the International School of the Bible,
Marietta, GA, U.S.A.
info@isob-bible.org   www.isob-bible.org


Copyright © 2008 by Larry Chkoreff- Author
Published by the International School of the Bible,
Marietta, Georgia, U.S.A.
Contributing-Editors - Michael and Karen Vincent

All rights reserved. This book is the sole property of the author. It may not be reproduced, altered, or transmitted in whole or in part without the express written consent of the author. Any unauthorized reproduction, alteration, transmission, or printing of this book, or any material contained in this book, is strictly prohibited. Permission to reproduce, alter, transmit, print or reprint this book, or any materials contained in this book, may be requested at the above email address. Any reference to the materials, ideas, or direct quotations taken from this book must be cited appropriately to this published edition.

Unless otherwise noted, Scripture quotations are from the NKJV of the Bible. Copyright 1979, 1980, 1982 by Thomas Nelson, publishers. Used by permission.

## Table of Contents

| | |
|---|---|
| INTRODUCTION | 7 |
| A SPECIAL NOTE FROM MICHAEL & KAREN VINCENT | 10 |
| CHAPTER 1 – A VISION TO BE HEALED | 16 |
| CHAPTER 2 – WHY DOES GOD RELEASE YOU? | 28 |
| CHAPTER 3 – POWER OF VISION - RELATIONSHIP SKILLS | 38 |
| CHAPTER 4 – WOUNDS FROM OTHERS | 50 |
| CHAPTER 5 – WOUNDS FROM GENERATIONAL CURSES | 66 |
| CHAPTER 6 – WOUNDS FROM OUR OWN SIN | 88 |
| CHAPTER 7 – JUDGMENTS AND VOWS | 105 |
| CHAPTER 8 – SOUL TIES | 118 |
| CHAPTER 9 – GRIEVING | 126 |
| CHAPTER 10 – FORGIVENESS | 139 |
| CHAPTER 11 – SCABS AND SCARS | 153 |
| CHAPTER 12 – SHAME - GUILT | 160 |
| CHAPTER 13 – THE WAR FOR YOUR THOUGHT LIFE | 175 |
| CHAPTER 14– LIVING LIKE WHO YOU REALLY ARE | 186 |
| CHAPTER 15– ARE YOU STILL STRUGGLING? | 198 |

| | |
|---|---|
| CHAPTER 16 – SPIRITUAL WARFARE | 201 |
| CHAPTER 17 – YOUR STONE IS ROLLED AWAY | 209 |
| APPENDIX A – RELATIONSHIP SKILLS | 219 |
| END NOTES | 223 |

# FORWARD

*Joel 2:25-26 (KJV) says, "And I will restore to you the years that the locust hath eaten, the cankerworm, and the caterpillar, and the palmerworm, my great army which I sent among you. And ye shall eat in plenty, and be satisfied, and praise the name of the LORD your God, that hath dealt wondrously with you: and my people shall never be ashamed."*

You may find the past years of your life wasted and consumed by your own sin and the sin perpetrated against you by others. Yet, as through a metamorphous, the caterpillar becomes a butterfly, so God provides a supernatural metamorphous, a transformation (metamorphoo in Greek), which can take place.

Through the prophet Joel, the Lord says that He will restore what was lost and consumed. God does not merely promise a better future; He actually promises to utilize your past devastation in such a way so as to transform the loss of the past to profit.

The butterfly does not even remember being a caterpillar. Nor will you even lament your devoured and wasted years. The Lord will cause your future to be fruitful in amazing ways. The caterpillar begins as a devourer, but becomes a useful and fruitful butterfly, an insect that has a productive purpose.

God spoke this verse to the author of this book, my husband Larry, shortly after he met Jesus in 1979. Larry had been lamenting his past wasted years. Now, many years later, he can testify to the truth and fulfillment of this promise.

This book presents some practical tools along with powerful truths for the healing of your inner and invisible wounds that may have come upon you by your sin and the sin of others. God's healing will make you a free person, able to "fly" and be fruitful as depicted by the butterfly on the front cover.

Carol Chkoreff
January 2009

## COMMENT

The tittle "FREE TO BE YOU" is appropriate because the *you* in you has been wounded and boxed with guilt. Now you can deconstruct your past and build for the future. The Israelites who came from Egypt left Egypt, but Egypt did not leave them. The problem has been how to get rid of the Egypt in them. Now here comes the inner healing nugget. Grab it and use it for yourself and others still reeling in pains. Choose freedom and divine health.

John Brown Okwii, PhD.
President,
The Apostolic Church LAWNA Theological Seminary Jos,
PL930001, Nigeria

## CREDITS

We have named Michael and Karen Vincent as *Contributing Editors* for lack of a better definition of their roles in this book. However, I feel that the importance of their contribution has been vital!

Karen Vincent certainly performed some very important basic editing. However, during the past six years (since 2003), both Michael and Karen taught me so much about inner healing from their own experiences and training that I feel that they are more than Contributing Editors. We have worked and ministered together on many occasions, and have recorded 18 video series named ISOB Bondage Breakers.

Also, while Michael and Karen were editing this book, I gave them total freedom to add their own testimonies and experiences. They added a lot of their own ideas into many parts of the text.

All the glory goes to Jesus, but also many thanks to Michael and Karen.

A word of great thanks goes to Tracey Diaz for the beautiful cover art.

Larry Chkoreff

# Free To Be You
## Introduction

Have you ever found yourself as a prisoner but you could not see the bars of the prison? Have you felt heavily weighed down inside? Have you fought depression? Do you ever feel like you are a victim to anger or fear, and you just don't know how to make it stop? Do you find yourself behaving in ways that you are ashamed of, but just cannot find the power to change? Do you walk into a group of friends or acquaintances, perhaps even at church, and say "fine" when they ask you how you are doing, and you know your are not telling the truth? Most of the time they don't want to know the truth. Do you find yourself addicted to drugs, alcohol, pornography, overeating, or any other such addiction? Are you tired of the "programs" that promise much but do not deliver?

My two contributing editors and I have been there, and we all have been set free! We will walk you down the paths that we have been on. We pray that your path will collide with God as ours did and that through applying the same biblical principles you will also be a free person.

**There is hope!**
Jesus, the Creator of the universe, came as a man into this world to give you the power to change and be free. His mission statement was prophesied in Isaiah chapter 61 hundreds of years before His birth. When He was ready to begin His earthly ministry He quoted a portion of that Isaiah Scripture.

"The Spirit of the Lord GOD *is* upon Me, Because the LORD has anointed Me To preach good tidings to the poor; He has sent Me to heal the brokenhearted, To proclaim liberty to the captives, And the opening of the prison to *those who are* bound; To proclaim the acceptable year of the LORD, And the day of vengeance of our God; To comfort all who mourn, To console those who mourn in Zion, To give them beauty for ashes, The oil of joy for mourning, The garment of praise for the spirit of heaviness; That they may be called trees of righteousness, The planting of the LORD, that He may be glorified." And they shall rebuild the old ruins, They shall raise up the former desolations, And they shall repair the ruined cities, The desolations of many generations" (Isaiah 61:1-4).

"And He was handed the book of the prophet Isaiah. And when He had opened the book, He found the place where it was written: 'The Spirit of the LORD *is* upon Me, Because He has anointed Me To preach the gospel to *the* poor; He has sent Me to heal the brokenhearted, To proclaim liberty to *the* captives And recovery of sight to *the* blind, To set at liberty those who are oppressed; To proclaim the acceptable year of the LORD.' Then He closed the book, and gave *it* back to the attendant and sat down. And the eyes of all who were in the synagogue were fixed on Him. And He began to say to them, 'Today this Scripture is fulfilled in your hearing'" (Luke 4:17-21).

*Notice He mentioned help for:*
The poor
The brokenhearted
The captives
The prisoners

The Acceptable Year of the Lord is the Year of Jubilee as stated in Leviticus chapter 25. That was the year when all debt was cancelled and the helpless debtors were set free.

He promised to bring sight to the blind. This includes the spiritually blind.

He said He could console those who mourn. Mourning is the emotional pain of grieving a loss. Most of us mourn inside because we have lost, or never have had, the "real us." We also may be mourning the loss of dreams and hopes, or maybe even the loss of a loved one.

**The problem is with the inner wounds that you cannot see.**
Humans are subject to being wounded in an invisible way, on the inside, in their souls. Most people, even many Christians, do not realize this, nor do they realize that Jesus came to heal these wounds and make their souls whole. Instead people with

wounded souls attempt to "medicate" their wounds with all kinds of ineffective "medications" instead of going to the One who heals. Some of these are drugs, alcohol, sexual addictions, religious attitude, or busyness. Others pour themselves obsessively into their work or fill their lives with worldly possessions as a means to medicate their wounds. Still others simply attempt to repress and bury the wounds through denial, and even become somewhat good at living a life that seems normal. But inside they feel oppressed and burdened, they know that something is terribly wrong, and they experience depression, anger and live without hope in emptiness.

Others live in a fantasy world where they always come out the winner because reality hurts too much. So they live in a fantasy, which keeps them in bondage from doing anything productive. I can testify that this was my case before Jesus saved me in 1979. Fantasy in one's mind is a dangerous thing. It is a real temptation to many people as a way of escape.

All of these attempts only hinder us from our true purpose and destiny in life.

**Make your decision now!**
If you have been discouraged over the years and now feel hopeless that you or God can do anything about your situation, then hear this. Do not read this book with the burden that you have to use your own strength one more time and experience one more failure. My question to you is this, will you just submit to developing your relationship with God and watch Him do the miracle in your life?

If you are not prepared to take the needed time daily, even hourly to keep your relationship with Jesus strong, then we recommend that stop here and give this book to someone else.

## A Special Note From the Contributing Editors Michael and Karen Vincent
## The Cross and Healing

The contributing editors Michael and Karen Vincent wrote the following comments about the Cross of Jesus and healing. They wrote this in order that you, the reader, might realize at the beginning of this book the wonderful gift and finished work accomplished for you by Jesus' suffering on the Cross in order to give you the gift of salvation from death.

If you meet this Jesus, He will cleanse you from your sin, heal your wounds and put you in a real relationship with Him. He will see that all your failures past, present and future will work together for your good.

The apostle Paul makes a statement in **Galatians 6:14(a) which says,** *"But God forbid that I should boast except in the cross of our Lord Jesus Christ..."*

What is the apostle Paul speaking of when he says the cross of Jesus Christ? He is speaking about the Lamb of God, Jesus Christ crucified, as our only savior. Paul had been a religious Pharisee; he persecuted and killed Christ followers. But when his eyes had been opened to who God truly was and what Jesus Christ had done for him he could only boast of the finished work of the cross of our Lord Jesus Christ. The cross of Jesus Christ is God's love toward sinners.

**Romans 6:23 says,** *"For the wages of sin is death, but the gift of God is eternal life in Christ Jesus our Lord."*

God being a holy God could not bring a sinful man like you and me, into relationship with Him and continue to be Holy. God would no longer be a just God if His justice were not fulfilled. As you can see we have a problem; but the answer is found in the cross. God humbled Himself and came down into this fallen world in the form of His son. He lived a sinless life and was obedient even to death upon a cross.

## Note From Michael & Karen Vincent

**2 Corinthians 5:21 says,** *"For He (God) made Him (Jesus Christ) who knew no sin to be sin for us, that we might become the righteousness of God in Him."*

Christ Jesus became every sin that has ever been or will ever be committed. Jesus took God's wrath in our stead.

**Isaiah 53:2 says,** *"For He (Jesus) shall grow up before Him as a tender plant, And as a root out of dry ground. He has no form or comeliness; And when we see Him, There is no beauty that we should desire Him."*

The prophet Isaiah was telling about the suffering and death to come. Jesus was beaten so bad that you could not even tell that He was a man. Have you ever seen a dried up root, how twisted and deformed it looks. He was disfigured for our sin. This is a picture of how horrible our sin looks to God. This is what our Lord looked like upon the cross. SIN!

Could you imagine what Jesus, the innocent Lamb of God was feeling, as He was turned into this dark, twisted, curse for sin. Every sin, past, present, and future was placed upon Him. Every lie, every curse, every thief, every lust, every fornication, every homosexual act, every rape, every fight, every anger, every covetousness, every gossip, every evil hidden sin that has ever been committed was placed upon the soul of the Son of God.

Think about how bad you feel about your sin, even with a harden heart, now think about how a pure sinless Lamb of God felt with all the sins of the world upon Him at once.

**Isaiah 53:10 says,** *"yet it pleased the Lord to bruise Him."*

Why did it please God to crush His own Son? Because He saw you, and He saw me, and He allowed His Son to take our place. The wrath we deserved, the death we deserved, Christ bore on that tree (For all have sinned and fallen short of the glory of God, and for the wages of sin is death.) Sin equals punishment, sin equals death and the wrath of a Holy and Just God was fulfilled upon the bosom of Christ. We will never understand the cost that He paid for our sins.

In all other religions we see the foundation based on the word "do," this is works. What we have to work for salvation. But in Christianity we see the word "**done**". Christ did everything on the cross and there is nothing we can do to add to it.

It is complete! It is finished!

**John 19:30 (b) says** *"He said, "It is finished!" And bowing His head, He gave up His spirit."*

God's wrath had been satisfied, and justice has been paid in full, all we have to do is believe.

**In Ephesians 2: 8-9 it says,** *"For by grace you have been saved through faith, and that not of yourselves; it is the gift of God,*

We are saved by faith and faith alone.

This is the good news of the gospel. What is the gospel? It is God's love through the birth, life, death, resurrection and ascension of Jesus Christ. The good news is Jesus Christ crucified as our only Savior.

**John 14:6 says,** *"Jesus said to him, I am the way, the truth and the life. No one comes to the Father except through me."*

I want to stop here for a moment, my beloved friends, maybe your eyes have been opened to the sinfulness of your life. You now see the miracle of what Jesus the innocent Lamb of God did for you upon the cross, taking your place, bearing your shame, taking your guilt, sin and nailing it to the cross. If you now see the life-blood of God's own Son shed for you, and you want everlasting life, stop and pray to God. Cry out to Him with all your heart, see His love for you, on the cross, repent and turn away from your sins and believe in Jesus Christ and you will be saved.

**Romans 10:9 says,** *"That if you confess with your mouth the Lord Jesus and believe in your heart that God has raised Him from the dead, you will be saved."*

If you just gave your heart to the Lord. I rejoice with the angels in heaven that your name is now written in the Lambs

## Note From Michael & Karen Vincent

Book of Life. If you are a child of God, and you have been born again, it is very important that you understand **Romans 8: 1-2 which says,**

*"1 There is therefore now no condemnation to those who are in Christ Jesus, who do not walk according to the flesh, but according to the Spirit.*

*2 For the law of the Spirit of life in Christ Jesus has made me free from the law of sin and death."*

I want to encourage you, as you go through this book, there is no shame. Christ bore all our shame. This is for freedom, where the Spirit of the Lord is there is freedom. We are not repenting of our sins to earn God's grace or love that would be the law of sin and death. But with a humble heart we are repenting because of God's grace and love, because He first loved us. This is the law of the Spirit of life in Christ Jesus.

This is inner healing, humility and truth. True humility is allowing God to show you the areas of your life that are not Christ-like. Sometimes our pain and fear causes us to live bound in unbelief that we are truly free. Inner healing is then going from the foot of the cross where we find salvation, (praise God) and taking the step forward in faith to climb upon the cross to be crucified with Christ. A dying to self. God's will not your will being done, this is the cup of the Lord Jesus Christ.

**Galatians 2:20 says,** *"I have been crucified with Christ; it is no longer I who live, but Christ lives in me; and the life which I now live in the flesh I live by faith in the Son of God, who loved me and gave Himself for me."*

Are you willing, in the grace of God, to humble yourself and pick up your cross? Jesus calls us to take up our cross.

**Luke 9:23 says,**

*"Then He said to them all, "If anyone desires to come after Me, let him deny himself, and take up his cross daily, and follow Me."*

This will not be easy. But it will be worth it. If you will trust the LORD, and move outside of your fear or religious thinking and allow the Holy Spirit to have His way it will bring about a life of peace and love that you cannot imagine.

The revival prophet Joel describes the heart of God in **Joel 2:12-13 which says,**

*"12 "Now, therefore," says the LORD, "Turn to Me with all your heart, With fasting, with weeping, and with mourning."*

*13 So rend your heart, and not your garments; Return to the LORD your God, For He is gracious and merciful, Slow to anger, and of great kindness; And He relents from doing harm."*

**Personal testimony from Michael Vincent.**

I share this not because I have learned this in my head, but in my heart, it is my life. See, for the first 37 years of my life I lived in fear, pain, unforgiveness, and shame. I believed everyone was better than me and I was a mistake. The last 21 years of this fearful life I medicated my wounded-ness with drugs, alcohol, and violence. For 21 years, I was in bondage to these demons. They had me to the point that all I could think about was suicide, in seemed to be my only way out. But in desperation I cried out to the Lord, and He heard me, came and saved me from the devil and myself, and gave me everlasting life. I have now been clean and sober for 12 years. But more than being clean and sober, I now know the love of the Father, and in this love I know who I am a beloved child of God. This is freedom! This is true living!

Fear and death know longer has power over me and I can allowed God into the deepest, darkest part of my heart to heal me. He has always been faithful. I have learned that I can trust Him. He has always accepted me right where I am. God has restored my marriage, my children, but most of all my relationship with Him. Now my wife Karen and myself can give God all the glory for what He has done!

**Romans 8:37-39 says,** *"Yet in all these things we are more than conquerors through Him who loved us.[38] For I am* *persuaded that neither death nor life, nor angels nor principalities nor powers, nor things present nor things to come, [39] nor height nor depth, nor any other created thing, shall be able to separate us from the love of God which is in Christ Jesus our Lord."*

# Chapter 1
## A Vision To Be Healed On The Inside

As an additional introduction to this book, I would like to begin by revealing an aspect of God's character and personality.

In Matthew chapter 12 verses 1-21 Jesus demonstrates one of God's most important attributes. He shows that God is more interested in people who are hurting than He is in rules and regulations.

**The Pharisees were giving Jesus a hard time about doing certain things on the Sabbath.**
When Jesus approached a man with a withered hand in their synagogue, the Pharisees again challenged Him asking if it was legal to heal a man on the Sabbath. In verse 12 Jesus said that this man was more valuable than animals that are rescued on the Sabbath. In verse 13 He said, "Stretch out your hand." The man's hand was restored as whole as the other. Now get this; the Pharisees plotted how they might destroy Jesus.

The real revelation comes in Matthew 12:18-21 which quotes a prophecy in Isaiah 42:1-3. "Behold! My Servant whom I have chosen, My Beloved in whom My soul is well pleased! I will put My Spirit upon Him, And He will declare justice to the Gentiles. He will not quarrel nor cry out, Nor will anyone hear His voice in the streets. *A bruised reed He will not break, And smoking flax He will not quench*, Till He sends forth justice to victory; And in His name Gentiles will trust" (Matthew 12:18-21).

*Children used to go to the riverbeds and cut off reeds in order to make flutes.* When they bruised the reed, they would not attempt to repair it. They could very easily discard it then go to the river and cut off another reed. The smoking flax was like the wick in an oil lamp. When it began to smoke instead of giving off clean light, they would simply cut off the wick that was smoking and cast it out.

My paraphrase on this is, "I do not throw people away just because they are bruised. They are invaluable to me. Just because your life has been bruised, just because your life is not reflecting the light of your God- given purpose, but is a smoking flax, I will not give up on you. I will come and heal the bruise and restore your life so that your light may again shine with the divine purposes of God. I will not cast you off, neither will your purpose be cut off. Healing your bruises will cause your flax to shine bright. Healing your inner bruises will cause you to ride upon the high places of your destiny and purpose in life."

Humans have a much more delicate psyche, spiritual and emotional make up than most of us realize. When God created Adam He created him for relationships. God told him to always eat from the Tree of Life, the Word of God, and to meet Him in the Garden. He brought Eve forth as a relationship companion of the highest type, except for Adam and God's. He created Adam to always be dependent on Him as a Father and provider.

When Adam and Eve preferred the Tree of Knowledge of Good and Evil, being their own talents and intellect without God's involvement, they fractured the most important relationship, that with their father, and they died. They died spiritually instantly, and eventually their bodies died.

*This break with their Father caused guilt, shame and self-rejection.* Eventually this sin was passed down to their children and to you and me as iniquity, or a liability with which we were born. This is called a generational curse.

**Broken relationships and dysfunctional families can even be found in Jesus' lineage.**

Dysfunction is passed down and the broken relationships compound throughout the generations. We find ourselves born into families that are full of broken relationships, or at least are reaping the iniquity of their forefather's iniquities. Many who live in a fatherless family find themselves sexually abused by father figures. Others have a father, but the mother will not allow the father to exercise their fatherly discipline; some are abused by their fathers.

As a result they find themselves living inexplicable lives. These include lifestyles that God never intended for his humans to experience. Perhaps we have eating addictions, drug and alcohol addictions, maybe we are perfectionists or religious legalists.

## Chapter 1 – A Vision To Be Healed On The Inside

These are all ways to attempt to "medicate" our inner wounds, which were really caused by broken relationships. It could be success or money that we use, or maybe inordinate sex and sexual relationships. Then we experience the fruit of these medications and broken relationships, some of which are shame, self-rejection, depression, anger, suicidal tendencies, hatred, selfishness, choosing to marry the wrong people for the wrong reasons, and the list goes on.

Some turn to religion, some to psychology and psychiatry, some to secular counseling. Others just drown in their medication methods, placing the blame everybody else, and live a life which is geared towards "Getting as much out of life as I can grab, happiness, adventure, success, money, power, etc."

It was a real revelation to me when I discovered that most of these human maladies are the result of one cause, that being broken relationships and the rejection associated with them, either past or present, especially with father figures. Considering that God's priority for us is a relationship with Him and good relations with others, it is no surprise that broken relationships cause all these problems.

Even with very good fathers and family background, if our relationship with our Heavenly Father is not right, we are liable to suffer many of the issues I have listed here.

## May we as the church minister God's healing with this in mind!

I pray that the Lord give us all His compassion for wounded people and that we would see them through His eyes as victims who need mercy and compassion.

The Hebrew Scriptures show us story after story of dysfunctional people. Look at Abraham, Isaac, Jacob, David, Moses, and the list goes on. Those stories show us real history. They also show us that God did not give up on His creation, although at times it got so bad that He had second thoughts. But He never gave up because He was not caught off guard. There are no "Oops" moments with God.

## Chapter 1 – A Vision To Be Healed On The Inside

The Hebrew Scriptures bring hope. They speak of a deliverer, a Messiah, who would come and bring the solution for this issue of a break with our fathers, and especially our Father God. They speak of the blood of a perfect lamb being shed to atone for sin.

Psalm 103 brings in hope, as it says in verses 1-4 and 12-13, "Bless the LORD, O my soul; And all that is within me, bless His holy name! Bless the LORD, O my soul, And forget not all His benefits: Who forgives all your iniquities, Who heals all your diseases, Who redeems your life from destruction, Who crowns you with lovingkindness and tender mercies." "As far as the east is from the west, So far has He removed our transgressions from us. As a father pities his children, So the LORD pities those who fear Him."

**A new and fresh look at types of forgiveness.**
Transgressions and iniquities affect us not only when enacted by us, but also when perpetrated against us by others. Notice God has a remedy for both those sins we commit and for those committed against us. Both are important. Some simply see forgiveness as something God does for us when we sin, but we will see it is much more as these chapters unfold.

**The remedy.**
Psalm 68 brings in healing hope for the break with the father relationship, which is really the key to our problem of rejection. "A father of the fatherless, a defender of widows, is God in His holy habitation. God sets the solitary in families; He brings out those who are bound into prosperity; But the rebellious dwell in a dry land" (Psalm 68:5-6). Here the Lord exposes Himself as One who understands our need to have a father/family relationship to be whole. It is amazing to see the unveiling of some people who looked like a lost cause and see their lives totally turned around because they saw God as their perfect Father.

Remember, Jesus bore our wounds of rejection by being rejected Himself by His Father on the Cross. "And at the ninth hour Jesus cried out with a loud voice, saying, 'Eloi, Eloi, lama

## Chapter 1 – A Vision To Be Healed On The Inside

sabachthani?' which is translated, 'My God, My God, why have You forsaken Me?'" (Mark 15:34).

God makes an amazing statement through His prophet Malachi in the final book of the Hebrew Scriptures, the Old Testament. "Behold, I will send you Elijah the prophet Before the coming of the great and dreadful day of the LORD. And he will turn [go back to the starting point] The hearts of the fathers to the children, And the hearts of the children to their fathers, Lest I come and strike the earth with a curse" (Malachi 4:5-6).

I have personally examined that Scripture for years looking for revelation. I kind of understood it, but I always had this desire to see more into it than I knew I was seeing. Looking into the Amplified Version and into the Hebrew words of this Scripture, it could be paraphrased as follows:

"I am going to send you people, who carry the name of Elijah, or in other words (what the name Elijah means), say of themselves, 'Jehovah is my God.' I will reveal My heart to these people, thus making them prophets of this revelation I am going to give to them. This revelation and their prophecy will be in the very face of and during the end-times sufferings and tribulations age (which we are now in). These people will proclaim My message to the ones who feel rejected by their father figures. That message is, 'Jesus My Son has taken your rejection because I rejected Him on the Cross. He bore that for you, therefore I can now turn My heart towards you with My love, and for many their response will be to turn their rebellious heart back to Me their true Father.'"

I don't have space to break that all down, but I feel that I have kept the meaning of the Hebrew translation.

***The angel told Zacharias, the father of John the Baptist, a similar message.*** "He will also go before Him in the spirit and power of Elijah, 'to turn the hearts of the fathers to the children,' and the disobedient to the wisdom of the just, to make ready a people prepared for the Lord" (Luke 1:17).

**Jesus performed a miracle as recorded in Mark chapter 2 that, I believe, tells that story better than any theology.**

Chapter 1 – A Vision To Be Healed On The Inside

**Mark 2:1-12 says,**
*1 And again He entered Capernaum after some days, and it was heard that He was in the house.*

*2 Immediately many gathered together, so that there was no longer room to receive them, not even near the door. And He preached the word to them.*

*3 Then they came to Him, bringing a paralytic who was carried by four men.*

*4 And when they could not come near Him because of the crowd, they uncovered the roof where He was. So when they had broken through, they let down the bed on which the paralytic was lying.*

*5 When Jesus saw their faith, He said to the paralytic, "Son, your sins are forgiven you."*

*6 And some of the scribes were sitting there and reasoning in their hearts,*

*7 "Why does this Man speak blasphemies like this? Who can forgive sins but God alone?"*

*8 But immediately, when Jesus perceived in His spirit that they reasoned thus within themselves, He said to them, "Why do you reason about these things in your hearts?*

*9 "Which is easier, to say to the paralytic, 'Your sins are forgiven you,' or to say, 'Arise, take up your bed and walk'?*

*10 "But that you may know that the Son of Man has power on earth to forgive sins" --He said to the paralytic,*

*11 "I say to you, arise, take up your bed, and go to your house."*

*12w Immediately he arose, took up the bed, and went out in the presence of them all, so that all were amazed and glorified God, saying, "We never saw anything like this!"*

**Notice in verse 5 when Jesus said, "Son."** The word "son" in Greek is teknon, which carries this meaning: "You who have been begotten by a father and family but have no relationship with

## Chapter 1 – A Vision To Be Healed On The Inside

either." Notice, this man's family did not bring him to Jesus, but four men who had faith. Jesus forgave him of his sins first, then addressed his broken relationship, and then came the healing.

**Notice in verse 11 what Jesus told him to do.** "I say to you, arise, take up your bed, and go to your house." I suggest that Jesus wanted this man to go and reconcile things with his family, forgive them, and even lead them to Jesus.

I believe that is a picture of a real church, using their faith to bring paralyzed people to Jesus. Would we just bring people to Jesus and let Him do the work instead of trying to fix them, which often leads to more wounds.

Teknon does not necessarily mean there is no relationship, it simply means one who has been begotten. I believe the implication by Jesus was as I have stated. There are other words Jesus could have used.

**You may not be paralyzed in body, but maybe in spirit or in lifestyle.** Maybe you are paralyzed to stop drugs, overeating, pornography, or any other obsessive behavior. Maybe you are eating to medicate your relationship emptiness; maybe you are doing destructive things to your body like cutting or other such painful acts. Maybe you cannot stop inordinate sex, looking at pornography, anger, depression, and the list goes on. Your external paralysis has an inner cure for which Jesus paid the ultimate price.

Then Jesus said, "your sins are forgiven you." In other words, those iniquities that have cut off your father/son and family relationship were borne by Me. Forgive means to cut away and take away. That rejection and relationship void that had made this man paralyzed has been borne by Jesus at the Cross. Jesus could have just as easily said, "Son, I am going to the cross in a few years and there My Daddy will turn His head and reject Me, so that this sin you have endured will be forgiven and taken away from you.

Isaiah 53:5 says that Jesus was bruised for our iniquities. Iniquities are an inner wound, as bruises are also inner wounds.

Chapter 1 – A Vision To Be Healed On The Inside

Jeremiah said, "In those days they shall say no more: 'The fathers have eaten sour grapes, And the children's teeth are set on edge.' But every one shall die for his own iniquity; every man who eats the sour grapes, his teeth shall be set on edge" (Jeremiah 31:29-30). In other words, in the New Covenant, Jesus will absorb that which could not be absorbed in the Old Covenant. The curses from former generations will not have to be suffered by you because Jesus suffered them in your stead.

***Look what happened!*** "Immediately he arose, took up the bed, and went out in the presence of them all, so that all were amazed and glorified God, saying, 'We never saw anything like this!'"

When you allow Jesus to go down deep and forgive those things done to you, or perhaps issues that were iniquities and were passed down to you by forefathers, and you agree with Him to issue that forgiveness, then your other issues will be resolved. Understanding this bigger picture about forgiveness will make it easier for you to forgive those who have hurt you or who have passed down iniquities to you.

***Healing starts from the inside and works its way out.***

There are ways in which we can cooperate with the Holy Spirit to allow Him to get down deep, underneath all of layers of "onion peels" to our inner wounds, and we will cover those in later chapters.

**Perpetrator or victim?**
So far we have been focusing on the victim of the rejection, and how this causes wounds in him or her. We also need to address the fact that the perpetrator of abuse and/or rejection can also receive mercy and forgiveness. Most likely, if you were or are a perpetrator, you have also been a victim. You may be feeling a lot of guilt and condemnation as you read this. You should feel a healthy guilt. However, you need not feel condemnation, or a final judgment. Your final judgment can and should be forgiveness through the work of Jesus Christ. Yes, He took your sin as well. He stands forgiving you and invites you to accept his forgiveness

## Chapter 1 – A Vision To Be Healed On The Inside

as you confess and repent and put yourself into His hands for healing. It may not feel like it comes immediately, but keep pressing in.

The night before I wrote this, a man I know came to me with a testimony. Actually, by the time I finished writing this chapter, there were three such testimonies. I knew that this man was a radical follower of Jesus, and I also knew that he had been in bondage to sexual sin. Even though a believer, he struggled to become completely free. He testified to me that his woundedness came to him from his father who did not raise him properly. However, because he forgave his father his father is now a radical follower of Jesus. He is a man who stays hungry for the Word. My friend told me that he now sees his father as a "King David" who committed horrible sins, but finally became a "Man after God's heart."

**Prosperity of the soul.**
*3 John 1:1-4 (Amplified Bible) says,*

*1 THE ELDERLY elder [of the church addresses this letter] to the beloved (esteemed) Gaius, whom I truly love.*

*2 Beloved, I pray that you may prosper in every way and [that your body] may keep well, even as [I know] your soul keeps well and prospers.*

*3 In fact, I greatly rejoiced when [some of] the brethren from time to time arrived and spoke [so highly] of the sincerity and fidelity of your life, as indeed you do live in the Truth [the whole Gospel presents].*

*4 I have no greater joy than this, to hear that my [spiritual] children are living their lives in the Truth.*

**Prosperity, as defined by The Strong's Concordance, means:**
*Easy to travel through, good, well and a good way, a good journey. To make prosperous, to be led in a prosperous journey, success. To bear fruit, to come to completion. Antonym: To suffer shipwreck, to fail.*

## Chapter 1 – A Vision To Be Healed On The Inside

This was not a promise to Gaius to whom this letter was written. It was rather the wish of the writer, John, in the same manner in which we would write saying, "I hope you are well and have all your needs met." In verse three, John adds to that hope the observation that when you are living your life in the Truth of whole Gospel you will prosper.

Prosperity and success in God's eyes are very different than the world's definition. God considers crucifixion as a success. He pre-ordained the crucifixion of Jesus for the salvation of whoever accepts it. He considers persecution, hardship, and sacrifice as success in His eyes. The important thing is not status, achievements, reputation, or profit. It is godly character and eternal fruit.

***Prosperity of the soul begins, as it states in verse 3 above, by "living in the Truth of the whole Gospel."***

We need to first anchor our beliefs in what Jesus did for us and who He made us to be. Then we need to act on that belief, as the word "believe" in the Bible is an action verb.

***Prosperity of the soul is made complete by taking up your cross for the three areas of you soul.***

***1. Will.*** Is Jesus really in control of your life? Have you made Him Lord? That is the condition of being saved, making Him Lord. Saved is to be delivered from danger.

***2. Mind.*** Do you take up your cross and take your ungodly thoughts captive and allow the Word of God to heal your mind?

***3. Emotions.*** Do you allow your emotions to control your life, or do you take up your cross and tell your emotions to get into the back seat?

***This is living your life in the Truth of the whole Gospel.*** This is the healing of your soul. The soul's prosperity will follow the taking up of your cross as defined above, and prosperity in your life will follow.

## Help in tough financial times.

Many people are brought to the "end of themselves" in the area of finances. It is through this door that Jesus brings many people to

## Chapter 1 – A Vision To Be Healed On The Inside

trust Him and His Father. I call this being changed through a felt-need. If you are unable to make life work financially, you are a candidate for healing just as this paralytic was in Mark chapter two.

Imagine this. The paralytic was unable to work and function in life. Not only was he dependent on others for his livelihood, but also he could not marry and have children. His self-esteem was most probably very low, and no doubt he was living without hope.

If you find yourself with this felt-need, then begin to live the "Overcoming lifestyle" that we will be describing in this book, and you will be converted from a *teknon* son/daughter (one who is merely born but with no intimate relationship), to a *huios* son/daughter as described in Revelation 21 below.

God shows us in Revelation that after we go through all of the tough times of standing on His Word in the face of tribulation, doubt and being tempted to not trust God, that the end of it will be a wonderful connection with God our Daddy, our Abba, provider.

"He who overcomes shall inherit all things, and I will be his God and he shall be My son" (Revelation 21:7). We inherit all things. We are no longer a son, teknon, a son without the intimacy of our Daddy, but in this Scripture son is translated *huios*.

### *Huios defined in Strong's Concordance.*

*Those who revere God as their father, those who in character and life resemble God, those who are governed by the Spirit of God, repose the same calm and joyful trust in God which children do in their parents (Rom. 8:14, Gal. 3:26), and hereafter in the blessedness and glory of the life eternal will openly wear this dignity of the sons of God. Term used preeminently of Jesus Christ, as enjoying the supreme love of God, united to him in affectionate intimacy, privy to his saving councils, obedient to the Father's will in all his acts.*

**My co-editors and I have amazing testimonies on how God, through our huios relationship with Him, has performed miracles in our finances and other felt-needs in life.**
I am talking about God coming through in our financial lives way beyond what our natural talents, abilities and opportunities could have produced. As we have gone through the inner healing process, it was almost a series of concurrent events that occurred in our financial realms. Businesses were formed, major debts were cancelled, funds came in for ministry, homes were purchased, and worry over the day to day finances vanished. We could see Jesus active in our lives taking care of our financial situations. We still see Him as the King of the Kingdom. We can testify that when we sought first His Kingdom and His righteousness, that all the things we needed were added (Matthew 6:33).

**What you may expect in the chapters to follow is our emphasis these main points:**
    1. Strengthening your personal relationship with your Father God, your true self, and others.
    2. Cooperating with God as He delicately uncovers our inner wounds and heals them, or in Bible vernacular, forgives them. It is all in the relationship!

# Chapter 2
# Why Does God Release You From Bondage?

We have been focusing on the healing of our inner wounds through forgiveness resulting in the release from bondages. We have proposed that our wounds have come from different types of sin; the sins against us by others like rejection or abuse, our own sin, and the generational sins that we inherit. We have seen how Jesus bore all these sins for us. He was wounded for our wounds, when we truly believe this and walk it out, we become free. However, we have also coupled with this that the reason for that release is that we can be in relationship with our Father God.

We have covered the idea that the love of God is the most powerful positive force and that rejection is the most powerful negative force. Rejection from a father, a father figure or perhaps even the inheritance of the generational curse of rejection, is a very powerful type of wound. This type of inner wound prevents us from our God-given purpose, which is to be in a tight real-time relationship with our Abba Father God.

## Why does God want us free?
Many people focus only on the "getting free" aspect and then fall short of the ultimate purpose, a relationship with Father God. The New Testament makes it clear that we were created to be a slave to somebody; we have no choice. Our only choice is we may be a slave to Satan or to Jesus and The Father. "Do you not know that to whom you present yourselves slaves to obey, you are that one's slaves whom you obey, whether of sin leading to death, or of obedience leading to righteousness?" (Romans 6:16).

*God wants us free so that we may choose Him, and live for Him.*

"...and He died for all, that those who live should live no longer for themselves, but for Him who died for them and rose again" (2 Corinthians 5:15).

God knows that the only way we can live a fruitful prosperous life is to live for Him. He loves us so much, that He wants us to live for Him, and in doing so we are looking after our own best interests.

## Lost dreams? Does your life feel without purpose?
*God wants you "Free To Be You."*

So many people, even believers, have lost (or have never even had) the dreams and visions for their life's purpose. God has hardwired you with a wonderful purpose in life, one that will be "abundant" in your eyes. He sets you free, not to be an independent person, but a person under the Lordship of Jesus Christ. The result is you will come out of your bondages and into a worship relationship with Him. You will inherit your original purpose for life and your God-given dreams will be revived and will come to reality. My co-editors and I have seen this happen in our lives. We all have seen God do things in our lives that are beyond comprehension, beyond our wildest dreams, that we could have not produced.

Ephesians 3:20 (Amplified Bible) says, "Now to Him Who, by (in consequence of) the [action of His] power that is at work within us, is able to [carry out His purpose and] do superabundantly, far over and above all that we [dare] ask or think [infinitely beyond our highest prayers, desires, thoughts, hopes, or dreams]."

## Take a lesson from the Egyptian bondage and exodus.
"Then you shall say to Pharaoh, 'Thus says the LORD: 'Israel is My son, My firstborn. So I say to you, let My son [God's Son Jesus was actually in Israel] go that he may *serve* Me. But if you refuse to let him go, indeed I will kill your son, your firstborn'" (Exodus 4:22-23).

Notice the word "serve." In Hebrew it is *abad*, which means to worship and even to work hard and work as a slave. Earlier in Exodus, God used that same word to indicate the type of bondage His people were in to Pharaoh. That does not mean that God is a hard taskmaster as Pharaoh was and Satan is, but it does infer that there is no middle ground of independence. There is no such thing as independence for man. You can only be free as a bondservant to Jesus the One who loves you and gave His life for you.

***God wanted His people free.***

He was going to take His action whether Pharaoh (Satan) or the people cooperated or not. Satan had no choice. God was going to disable the enemy and set His people free, however, then it was up to them to take the next step and "*serve*" Him, or to be in fellowship with Him as their Father God.

God not only asked them to serve Him, but He also wanted them to "sacrifice." "Then they will heed your voice; and you shall come, you and the elders of Israel, to the king of Egypt; and you shall say to him, 'The LORD God of the Hebrews has met with us; and now, please, let us go three days' journey into the wilderness, that we may *sacrifice* to the LORD our God'" (Exodus 3:18).

Now put yourself into the culture of God and His definition of relationship. Sacrifice means to die. It infers blood covenant. There is no relationship with God (or in marriage) outside of a blood covenant, and there can be no blood covenant without death by both parties. In today's terms, we are to "take up our cross daily" in order to truly relate to God. We do not shed physical blood, but the blood of our old soul life, the unregenerate selfish person we were before we met Jesus. We will soon see how God Himself shed His blood for this relationship.

***Moses reached his wit's end.***

He told God in Exodus 5:22-23 that ever since he approached Pharaoh with God's message of letting His people go, Pharaoh did not let them go but he increased their suffering.

God answered. "Then the LORD said to Moses, 'Now you shall see what I will do to Pharaoh. For with a strong hand he will let them go, and with a strong hand he will drive them out of his land.' And God spoke to Moses and said to him: 'I am the LORD. I appeared to Abraham, to Isaac, and to Jacob, as God Almighty [El Shaddai], but by My name LORD [Jehovah] I was not known to them. I have also established My covenant with them, to give them the land of Canaan, the land of their pilgrimage, in which they were strangers. And I have also heard the groaning of the

## Chapter 2 – Why Does God Release You From Bondage?

children of Israel whom the Egyptians keep in bondage, and I have remembered My covenant'" (Exodus 6:1-5).

***First, God was going to turn His attention to the enemy, and then, when the enemy was disabled, God would concentrate on His relationship with His people.*** Notice in the Exodus 6:1-5 God said that He was going to appear for the first time with a different name. Instead of El Shaddai He would appear as Jehovah, the bondage breaker. The name Jesus means, "Jehovah is salvation." What God was saying was, "You knew Me as God Almighty, but now I am going to show you My other side, I am Jesus the bondage breaker. You will see Me shed blood to set you free!"

***God was bringing His Son on the scene to set His people free so that they would go and serve Him, the Father.***

Jesus always pointed us to the Father. Jesus said that He was the Way to the Father. It is the same in this Exodus story. Jehovah was the bondage breaker so that the people could go worship, sacrifice and be in relationship with their Father. Even if we are too bound up to accept God's bondage breaker power He still moves ahead.

"So Moses spoke thus to the children of Israel; but they did not heed Moses, because of anguish of spirit and cruel bondage" (Exodus 6:9). This shows how the bondage of many generations affected the Israelites.

From Exodus chapter 7 and following, God started putting the plagues on the gods of Egypt. The tenth and final plague was the Passover. This represents the Cross, the blood of Jesus, the blood covenant. This represents God's entire wrath put on the Lamb of God. The Passover represents forgiveness. This represents disarming Pharaoh and Satan because all sin was forgiven. In other words, whatever you did wrong and whatever wrongs were done to you were put on Jesus. He was bruised for your iniquities. Your rejection was put on Jesus at the Cross.

The people were now free to go into the wilderness to worship, sacrifice and serve their Father Creator. "Then he called for Moses and Aaron by night, and said, 'Rise, go out from among my people, both you and the children of Israel. And go, serve the

LORD as you have said'" (Exodus 12:31). God instructed the people to hurry out of Egypt even before their bread could leaven. When we see that we have been set free, it is our choice to run from our old bondage to go build our relationship with our Father.

***Only two of the original group made it to the Promised Land.***

"...except Caleb the son of Jephunneh, the Kenizzite, and Joshua the son of Nun, for they have wholly followed the LORD" (Numbers 32:12). "For the LORD had said of them, 'They shall surely die in the wilderness.' So there was not left a man of them, except Caleb the son of Jephunneh and Joshua the son of Nun" (Numbers 26:65).

In looking at the Book of Numbers it is obvious that Joshua and Caleb spent more time around the Tabernacle then the masses. They had faith when it came to spying the land. Since faith only comes by hearing God speak, they must have been in contact with Him. Moses didn't make it for a different reason. As God's representative his responsibility was greater. He misrepresented God's character when he struck the rock inferring that God was mad with them.

***There are only two choices for you.***

Those two choices are to get into a deep abiding relationship with Jesus, or die in the wilderness. That is why we stress the relationship skills so much. Approximately 2,000,000 people fled the bondage in Egypt, and of those all but two died in the wilderness. Those two, Joshua and Caleb spent time around the Tabernacle; they pursued the relationship with God with great zeal.

**How did God expect them to make it from Egypt to the Promise land, knowing there was a desert with no water, no food, enemies they would have to go to war with, and even giants that would instill fear in them?**

*How does He expect us to make the same journey after we meet Him?*

## Chapter 2 – Why Does God Release You From Bondage?

God gave them and us a vision of the Cross and resurrection of Jesus in order to keep our minds focused on truth throughout our sufferings!

**Exodus 15:22-16:3 says,**

*"22 So Moses brought Israel from the Red Sea; then they went out into the Wilderness of Shur. And they went three days in the wilderness and found no water.*

*23 Now when they came to Marah, they could not drink the waters of Marah, for they were bitter. Therefore the name of it was called Marah.*

**(Marah means bitter.)**

*24 And the people complained against Moses, saying, "What shall we drink?"*

*25 So he cried out to the LORD, and the LORD showed him a tree. When he cast it into the waters, the waters were made sweet. There He made a statute and an ordinance for them. And there He tested them,*

**(The tree represented the Cross, which made the bitter turn sweet. Notice Moses did not just choose any tree, but God showed him which one to throw into the bitter waters.)**

*26 and said, "If you diligently heed the voice of the LORD your God and do what is right in His sight, give ear to His commandments and keep all His statutes, I will put none of the diseases on you which I have brought on the Egyptians. For I am the LORD who heals you."*

*27 Then they came to Elim, where there were twelve wells of water and seventy palm trees; so they camped there by the waters.*

**(Elim means Palms. Notice there were twelve wells of water. The number twelve refers to the Kingdom of God. They had shade and water, and food, either coconuts or dates.**

**This was to be a vision of how the Cross of Jesus would turn each and every trial they would face in the**

## Chapter 2 – Why Does God Release You From Bondage?

*Wilderness and with their enemies, into an Elim; the Kingdom of God.)*

*1 And they journeyed from Elim, and all the congregation of the children of Israel came to the Wilderness of Sin, which is between Elim and Sinai, on the fifteenth day of the second month after they departed from the land of Egypt.*

*2 Then the whole congregation of the children of Israel complained against Moses and Aaron in the wilderness.*

*3 And the children of Israel said to them, "Oh, that we had died by the hand of the LORD in the land of Egypt, when we sat by the pots of meat and when we ate bread to the full! For you have brought us out into this wilderness to kill this whole assembly with hunger.""*

*As you encounter sufferings in your "desert experience," keep your mind focused on the Tree that went into the bitter water, and how they went from the bitter to the sweetness of Elim. Keep your brain and mind focused on the Cross by reading about it in the Word, meditating upon it, and speaking it out.*

**Jesus provided the sacrifice to make us free people.**
However, it is our choice to respond to the blood covenant relationship He has established with our Father. Without pursuing that relationship we will remain in bondage!

It has been said, "Insanity is doing the same thing over and over again and expecting different results." If we do not develop our relationship skills with our Father as Joshua and Caleb did, we will remain in different types of bondages.

*Our discipline is not some sort of legalism or self help program, but we do have to do our part.*

While we cannot discipline ourselves to stop a habit or make ourselves conform to the image of Christ, there is a discipline that we must observe. We need to learn new relationship skills. If we have not been used to these skills, practicing them will be our discipline. We were created for relationship especially with our Father God. Engaging in this relationship will bring supernatural consequences into our lives. This closeness to God will transfer His character and other fruit into our lives without effort. His power will supercharge us! Our effort is to maintain the relationship and to stand against the enemy.

Jesus said in John chapter 17 that eternal life is indeed *"knowing"* Him and His Father. *Knowing* is a relationship description. Paul said in Philippians chapter three that his passion was to *know* Jesus. He even stated that it would be worth all of the suffering just to know even the power of His resurrection even while in his earthly body. I can testify that so much of my *knowing* has been on the heels of "death and resurrection" experiences in my life.

**A God-given vision brings self-discipline.**
"Where *there is* no revelation, the people cast off restraint; But happy *is* he who keeps the law" (Proverbs 29:18). Studies of successful people in all walks of life, from brain surgeons to manual laborers, show that the one common element in all of them was self-discipline. It was not so much a self-discipline of vowing to not do something, as it was a disciple of doing something positive.

The apostle Paul had suffered from one of the worst addictions of all, that of being self-righteous. His vision and passion of knowing Christ as stated in Philippians chapter three is what released Paul from this horrible addiction. It will do the same for you. Will you have to utilize a certain amount of self-disciple against the negative? Yes. That will help break habits. However, replacing the negative with the positive is discipline that will allow God's power to really deliver you.

Peter set forth several positive disciplines for us in 2 Peter chapter 1:5-9. Then in verse 10 he said, "Therefore, brethren, be even more diligent to make your call and election sure, for if you do these things you will never stumble" (2 Peter 1:10).

## Chapter 2 – Why Does God Release You From Bondage?

**Relationship skills.**
Mankind has all but lost relationship skills. Our relationships are God's top priority.

If you have a great relationship with Jesus and our Father, then just let these following suggestions be a reminder to sharpen them. If you are in the process of developing that relationship, then perhaps these will give you some structure.

***We must meet God in the arena of truth.***

Jesus is the Truth; the Holy Spirit is the Spirit of Truth. I submit that there are two main realms of truth.

***First, our truth is where we are located.***

It is recognizing our own infirmities, faults, sins, pride, feelings, unforgiveness and perhaps even judgments against God. We must bring those before the Cross of Jesus and be honest with Him. As we do, we are forgiven and cleansed (1 John 1:9). We take up our cross when we struggle with continual repentance, not being satisfied with those parts of our lives that are out of Christ's character. Let us make sure we are not blaming others and justifying ourselves, but rather confessing our sins to one another that we may be healed.

At the same time we can recognize that there is no condemnation (Romans 8:1-2) as we continue with our walk of faith in the Spirit with our Father and Jesus. 1 Corinthians 11:31 says, "For if we would judge ourselves, we would not be judged."

***Second, Real Truth is the Word of God.***

The Word of God is Jesus. The Word of God is supernatural, it is the container of the blood covenant with God, and it is the primary means of hearing God and fellowshipping with Him. The Word will conform us to His image as it plants supernatural seeds. It brings faith to us. We connect to God through Jesus the Word.

The Word taken in and spoken out will cause Satan and his demons to flee from your lives and circumstances. As we speak the Word from the abundance of our hearts our minds are renewed and God is given authority to loose angels and all of His power on our behalf.

Chapter 2 – Why Does God Release You From Bondage?

**We offer resources for these relationship skills if you need them.**
[1] The Flowing River is a chapter in our Grow or Die book[2]. It gives a suggested set of relationship skills based upon God's Old Testament Tabernacle. This teaching has helped many people improve their own personal relationship skills with God. We have utilized much of the Flowing River lesson in a later chapter in this book. The Flowing River is a wonderful and simple discipline into the presence of God. [3] The Daily Moral Inventory is widely used by people who are serious about asking God to show them what areas they need to surrender to Him. A web link to that sheet is attached at the end of this chapter.

Please bear in mind that your relationship is personal and is not a formula. So please just take these skills as ideas and as an outline.

Our next chapter is dedicated to these Relationship Skills.

---

[1] Web link for the Flowing River http://www.isob-bible.org/flowingriver.htm
[2] Web link for Grow or Die book. http://www.isob-bible.org/component/content/article.html?id=292
[3] Web link for Daily Moral Inventory http://www.isob-bible.org/innerheal/moralinventory.htm

# Chapter 3
# The Power of Vision
## Relationship Skills

I want to plant a vision in your heart that will give you a powerful craving to strengthen your relationship with God.

A relationship with God through Jesus Christ and the Holy Spirit will bring peace, freedom and prosperity of all kinds, and most of all, will bring you into an intimate real-time fellowship with Jesus. He will become more and more real to you; you will feel and hear Him speak to you on a regular basis. However, such a relationship requires some real discipline on your part. All relationships require discipline, but when it's all in place, relationships are the most satisfying things we can enjoy.

**Vision brings discipline**.
"Where *there is* no revelation [vision], the people cast off restraint [discipline]; But happy *is* he who keeps the law" (Proverbs 29:18).

*The human psyche has been created to operate on vision, or in other words, hope.*

The first thing God said to Adam, as a way of blessing them, was to speak vision.

"Then God blessed them, and God said to them, 'Be fruitful and multiply; fill the earth and subdue it; have dominion over the fish of the sea, over the birds of the air, and over every living thing that moves on the earth'" (Genesis 1:28).

While this book is majoring on becoming free from the bondages that are manifested in ungodly lifestyles, you will see, as you read on, that the true bottom-line issue is improving your relationship with God. That and that alone will make you a free person.

Developing and improving your relationship with God requires discipline on your part. God has done everything, now it is your task to appropriate His wonderful work though an intimate relationship with Him.

Discipline requires a vision as it is stated in Proverbs 29:18. Most people realize that in order to succeed a vision is needed.

## Chapter 3 – The Power of Vision – Relationship Skills

When a doctor gives you a medicine, you go through the discipline of taking it because you have a vision of being healed.

When you report for work each day, you do the work even if you do not like it, because you have a vision of being paid.

When you go to the field and perform the hard task of reaping the harvest, you do it because you have a vision of eating.

I would like to cast a vision in your heart that I pray will cause you (and me) to become more disciplined with our relationship skills with God. Just look at the promises listed below for such discipline.

### 1. The vision for peace and freedom.
*2 Peter 1:2 (Amplified Bible) says,*
"May grace (God's favor) and peace (which is perfect well-being, all necessary good, all spiritual prosperity, and freedom from fears and agitating passions and moral conflicts) be multiplied to you in [the full, personal, precise, and correct] knowledge of God and of Jesus our Lord."

Notice, all of these wonderful benefits come through knowing God personally.

### 2. The vision for godly prosperity.
"Beloved, I pray that you may prosper in all things and be in health, just as your soul prospers. For I rejoiced greatly when brethren came and testified of the truth *that is* in you, just as you walk in the truth. I have no greater joy than to hear that my children walk in truth" (3 John 1:2-4).

Notice, prosperity in temporal matters is a result of your soul's prosperity. The prosperity of your soul comes by maintaining an intimate relationship with God.

Prosperity in God's eyes is very different than the world's definition. God sees crucifixion as a success. He pre-ordained the crucifixion of Jesus for the salvation of whoever accepts it. He considers persecution, hardship, and sacrifice as success in His eyes. The important thing is not status, achievements, reputation, or profit. It is godly character and eternal fruit. The word prosperity in the New Testament means to have a good journey.

If the journey includes hardships one might say this is not a good journey. However if the Cross of Jesus converts that hardship into a resurrected blessing for you and the Kingdom of God, then indeed the journey was not only good, it was fantastic.

*"God's promises are like the stars; the darker the night, the brighter they shine.*
DAVID NICHOLAS"

## 3. The vision for intimacy; God becoming real to you.
***Ephesians 3:17-19 (Amplified Bible) says,***

*"May Christ through your faith [actually] dwell (settle down, abide, make His permanent home) in your hearts! May you be rooted deep in love and founded securely on love, That you may have the power and be strong to apprehend and grasp with all the saints [God's devoted people, the experience of that love] what is the breadth and length and height and depth [of it]; [That you may really come] to know [practically, through experience for yourselves] the love of Christ, which far surpasses mere knowledge [without experience]; that you may be filled [through all your being] unto all the fullness of God [may have the richest measure of the divine Presence, and [d]become a body wholly filled and flooded with God Himself]!"*

***Philippians 3:10 says,***
*"that I may know Him and the power of His resurrection, and the fellowship of His sufferings, being conformed to His death."*

Notice that God becoming real to you is mostly about His amazing love for you personally. It may be hard to imagine, but God compares His love for you as a bridegroom longing for His bride! Do you feel unworthy? Drop it. Your Bridegroom is longing for you!

## 4. The vision to be like Jesus and be clean.
### 2 Peter 1:3-4 says,
*"as His divine power has given to us all things that pertain to life and godliness, through the knowledge of Him who called us by glory and virtue, by which have been given to us exceedingly great and precious promises, that through these you may be partakers of the divine nature, having escaped the corruption that is in the world through lust"*

Notice in the above Scripture that "knowing" God will bring us everything we need for life (our temporal needs) and godliness (our character).

## 5. The vision for fulfillment of your calling, purpose, and eternal rewards.
### 2 Timothy 1:9 says,
*"who has saved us and called us with a holy calling, not according to our works, but according to His own purpose and grace which was given to us in Christ Jesus before time began"*
### *Hebrews 11:6 says,*
*"But without faith it is impossible to please Him, for he who comes to God must believe that He is, and that He is a rewarder of those who diligently seek Him"*
### 2 Corinthians 5:10 says,
*"For we must all appear before the judgment seat of Christ, that each one may receive the things done in the body, according to what he has done, whether good or bad"*
### *1 Corinthians 9:25 says,*
*"And everyone who competes for the prize is temperate in all things. Now they do it to obtain a perishable crown, but we for an imperishable crown"*
### *Revelation 22:12 says,*

Chapter 3 – The Power of Vision – Relationship Skills

> *"And behold, I am coming quickly, and My reward is with Me, to give to every one according to his work"*

You may feel like purpose in life and eternal rewards are so far fetched compared to what you are experiencing now. You may feel like if you could just be healed from the inner wounds that are causing you pain that would be enough. The good news is that the two go together. Your healing in the present circumstances will bring God's best plan into your life for eternity.

I cannot explain everything about eternal rewards, but the Bible is clear about their existence. I do know that to abandon yourself totally to God in every area of your life is the ingredient God needs to bring you into His purpose, and thus eternal rewards.

T. Austin Sparks, an influential writer in the mid 1900s, covers this subject well in his book, Revelation of Jesus Christ. [4] One small quote from his book makes this clear.

*"He is over all. And that brings, whether world persecution or not, it brings spiritual conflict, it brings tribulation into the life. It touches us everywhere, in our families, in our homes, in our businesses and everywhere this thing is touching us; if only, if only we would let go something, make some compromise, let down our standard, not be so utter for Christ. We'd have an easier time, it is possible, you can, CAN for the time being! But you cast away your crown."*

**Vision from God brought Gideon from bondage to freedom, to purpose and prosperity.**

Gideon was living a defeated life as an Israelite until God gave him vision. He had a very low self-esteem because Israel's enemies had been prevailing. He had a wrong image of himself. God knew how His own power could and would change Gideon; however, He needed to change Gideon's own self-image. God spoke those

---

[4] Excerpt From: T. Austin-Sparks. "Revelation of Jesus Christ." iBooks. https://itun.es/us/-HcGF.l

things that were not as though they were. The more we fellowship with God, the more He is able to give us His accurate self-image of how He sees us. How He sees us is the truth, not how we feel about ourselves. That is hope, vision!

**Judges 6:12 says,**
*"And the Angel of the LORD appeared to him, and said to him, 'The LORD is with you, you mighty man of valor!'"*

Then in the next few chapters in Judges you will see that Gideon and God slowly but surely developed a deep personal relationship. That resulted in Gideon being clothed with the Holy Sprit and being able to hear God at a very intimate level. Then God used him to overthrow the enemy that had he and his people in bondage.

**Your task.**
I suggest that you meditate upon the Scriptures I listed above, speak them out, memorize them, and allow them to go deep into your heart and soul.

Then begin to engage in the Relationship Skills as suggested in Appendix A. If you are just starting take small steps. These small steps will build up momentum in your relationship skills.

Momentum makes the next step easier. Think of an automobile, it takes less energy to move the vehicle from 25 miles per hour to 40 miles per hour than it does to move it from 0 to 10 miles per hour. This is called the law of inertia. In even simpler terms, inertia means, "A body in motion tends to remain in motion, a body at rest tends to remain at rest." Also, the body in motion tends to keep on the same course, while change requires great effort.

If you are "at rest" and not moving in your relationship skills with God, then use the energy of your discipline to get on the proper course. If you do not have the passion for this relationship, or the passion for the Word of God, then confess that to the Lord and ask Him to do a new work in you.

## Relationship Skills
**1. Make a firm decision to pursue the relationship.** Offer yourself completely to God. This is our task to complete the mighty blood covenant offered to us by an awesome God. When we were born again our "old self" was crucified and it died. We were given a new nature; we are now new creations, returned to "normal" because now the Mighty God dwells in us. It is Him and Him alone that lives in us! The only remnant of the "old self" is in our thinking process. We have to continually renew our minds to these facts.

As we do, we will not be so aware of the demands of the "old self," which are always selfish. That selfishness causes fear, anger, control over circumstances, and many other horrible feelings.

I like to do this. As my "self" rises up, I say to it, "Get back to the grave, you are dead! I am not going to engage in fear and worry. I am not going to have to be noticed and praised."

*Meditate on these Scriptures.*
**Romans 12:1, 2 says,**
*"1 I beseech you therefore, brethren, by the mercies of God, that you present your bodies a living sacrifice, holy, acceptable to God, which is your reasonable service.*

*2 And do not be conformed to this world, but be transformed by the renewing of your mind, that you may prove what is that good and acceptable and perfect will of God."*

**Galatians 2:20 says,**
*"20 "I have been crucified with Christ; it is no longer I who live, but Christ lives in me; and the life which I now live in the flesh I live by faith in the Son of God, who loved me and gave Himself for me."*

**Romans 6:6 says,**
*"6 knowing this, that our old man was crucified with Him, that the body of sin might be done away with, that we should no longer be slaves of sin."*

## Chapter 3 – The Power of Vision – Relationship Skills

**Matthew 6:33 says,**
*"33 "But seek first the kingdom of God and His righteousness, and all these things shall be added to you."*

**2. Take time to listen: You must take in His Word**. Words are blood covenant containers. The Word of God is Jesus Himself; it is not a book of promises to pick and choose from. The Word of God should be pursued as a regular and daily relationship skill and should be looked at as listening to your Lord, Jesus Himself. Ask Him to speak. The Word is supernatural and it produces faith in the same way natural food produces energy. Jesus said that He is the true manna that gives eternal life. Write down what you feel He is speaking.

*Ways to discern whose voice you are hearing.*
God's voice: Affirms, corrects, direction (truth).
Satan's voice: Keeps us bound in failure with lies and condemnation.
Self's voice, or our flesh: justifies, rationalizes, denies and projects or blames others.

*Testing to see if we are hearing God's voice.*
Is it scriptural?
Does it glorify Jesus?
Is there a witness in my spirit?
Does it edify or tear down?
Does it produce freedom or bondage?

*Ways God speaks to us.*
The Bible. Revelation knowledge through the Holy Spirit.
The Body of Christ: Fellow believers, pastors, counselors. Be careful to not depend solely on this.
Quiet time: Holy Spirit's voice. (Psalm 139:23-24, 1 John 1:9).
Circumstances and situations in everyday life (Jeremiah 32:8).
Accountability Partner: Often it is wise to have a trusted friend who will be bold enough to hold you accountable for issues in your life.

**3. Take time to speak: Your words and prayer.** Two-way journaling and being gut-level honest is an important way to increase your relationship with God. Write down exactly how you feel. Honesty with your blood covenant partner Jesus will cause your sin to go on Him. You cannot and will not overcome any issue in life without this gut-level honesty. We suggest two-way journaling. This is a great way to allow the "flow" of the Holy Spirit to speak to you personal and intimate things. First, get in a quiet place, set your mind on Jesus, and begin to worship Him. You write down what you want to tell or ask Jesus. Then write down what you hear in your spirit. At first, there may be some mistakes, but through faith and practice, He will be real to you.

*Repentance is extremely important. Without repentance you will not be able to hear God speak.*
**Proverbs 1:23-24 Amp. Bible says,**
*If you will turn (repent) and give heed to my reproof, behold, I [Wisdom] will pour out my spirit upon you, I will make my words known to you.*

*Repentance is part of a healthy prayer life.*
**Matthew 26:41 says,**
*Watch and pray, that ye enter not into temptation: the spirit indeed is willing, but the flesh is weak.*

The visions I have listed in this chapter must be made personal to you. You can try to know them intellectually, but the Holy Spirit must eventually light them during an intimate time with the Lord.

Even then we are constantly tempted by our flesh nature. Satan sees that and strategizes how to cause us to lose our vision by having the temptation become real sin.

The word "enter" that Jesus used in Matthew 26:41 is inferred in the Strong's translation as to actually be overtaken by that temptation. It even infers Satan's activities. Jesus was tempted, but He prayed so as not to have that temptation become sin.

So prayer is absolutely vital. You will not make it without

prayer. There are many types of prayer. Sure we must ask, worship, be thankful, but we also must confess our sins. That even includes our temptations so that they do not actually "enter" us and thereby cut off our living relationship with Jesus at least for the time being. I have learned to simply confess all my temptations as if they were sin just to make sure. It has really been powerful!

*Gut level repentance is a key to maintaining the intimacy with God.*

Often we try to please God by our performance in doing good and even godly things. While that has its place and our efforts have good motives, it is usually not enough to maintain the intimacy. Colossians chapter 2 and 3 give us some ideas about this.

**Colossians 2:23 says,**

*"23 These things indeed have an appearance of wisdom in self-imposed religion, false humility, and neglect of the body, but are of no value against the indulgence of the flesh."*

At look at Colossians 3 gives us a better way. It is to "put off the old man" and "put on the new man," that is Christ who is in us. We can only do that by confessing our sin, and even our temptations to sin, and our ungodly behavior to Him. That intimacy is the only way to "put on Christ."

Keeping the honesty with God through your honest repentance is like keeping a marriage relationship strong. We must "take up our cross daily," and sacrifice ourselves to God. Remember the great sacrifice He made for us just to have the intimacy.

**4. Take time to speak: His Words.** The antagonist, Satan, and his assigned demons constantly are on task to come against your effort to relate to Jesus and to overcome. Only you can resist them. Jesus gave you the authority and responsibility to speak His Word against them. God told Joshua in Joshua 1:8, "This Book of the Law shall not depart from your mouth, but you shall meditate in it day and night, that you may observe to do according to all that is written in it. For then you will make your way prosperous, and then you will have good success."

***One idea for doing this is:***

Read Psalms and Proverbs by the day. You should read ALOUD five Psalms every morning. Use the system of the calendar, i.e., on the 3rd of the month read Psalms 3, 33, 63, 93 and 123. Also read Proverb 3. In this system the student will read all Psalms and Proverbs every month. Using this system renews the mind, speaks the Word to Satan, and allows the suffering student to relate his/her emotions to the Psalmist's. Provisions can be made for months with 31 days, and for Psalm 119.

Also be sensitive to the Holy Spirit Who will give you a Word of warfare for a particular situation.

**5. Meditation.** Meditation on the Word is very important and extremely valuable. I quoted Joshua 1:8 above which tells us to meditate day and night. Psalm 1:2-3 says, "But his delight *is* in the law of the LORD, And in His law he meditates day and night. He shall be like a tree Planted by the rivers of water, That brings forth its fruit in its season, Whose leaf also shall not wither; And whatever he does shall prosper."

Meditation on the Word displaces and replaces your carnal thinking which is a major feat. It also allows the Word to get down deep into your heart. The word meditate is related to a cow chewing her cud. She chews it, swallows it, regurgitates it, and then starts the process over again, and again, and again. This will allow the Word to go deeply into your heart, and will give the Holy Spirit an opportunity to speak something personal to you from the Word. I believe that meditation on those Scriptures that deal with the Cross and resurrection of Jesus is extremely valuable, especially when we are going through trials and suffering.

**6. Fasting.** Fasting is an important discipline. There are many types of fasts, and I will not cover that subject here. The main advantage of fasting is that it denies the strongest desire of the flesh, to eat. In doing so one is able to hear the Holy Spirit better.

Remember, the flesh lusts against the Spirit and the Spirit against the flesh, Galatians 5:17. I have read that when a person is hungry, even his/her natural hearing is better.

**7. Obey God**. Ask God to give you something simple, something small every day that you may obey. It may be just encouraging another, it may be not driving down the same street that fed your addiction; it may be confessing your sin to Him. It may be taking a thought captive, or forgiving someone, or perhaps giving a financial gift.

*This is a big thing!* John 14:21-23 says that when we obey His Word that He will reveal more and more of Himself to us. Once you have "seen" Jesus, relationship with Him will no longer be a discipline, but it will be a passionate pursuit.

# Chapter 4
# Wounds From Others

The first few chapters of this book were intended to give you a quick and simple understanding of wounds, their effects, and cures. We want to encourage you that God desires to heal you and that He will use a close relationship to Him to do so. We will now show you about the various causes of these wounds and pray that as you read you may be enlightened by the Holy Spirit to recognize such wounds within yourself.

I am not proposing to be an expert on the subject of inner wounds, abuse, and inner healing. However, I have learned some things about these subjects from my own experience and deliverance, from the Word of God, from the [5] Inner Healing book, and from my co-editors Michael and Karen. This book is not meant to be a complete clinical manual for inner healing; rather, it is intended to bring you the primary facts about wounds and the primary means of healing them. We believe that God will use our basic understanding and simple style of writing to encourage you, perhaps a simple believer, to pursue wholeness.

**Encouragement**.
I would like to give an encouraging word to you if perhaps you were abused, rejected or wounded in some way by another person or just by life itself. I want to encourage you if you are struggling with a habit, addiction or an ungodly lifestyle. As we progress further into future chapters, you will be given the solution to your problem, no matter how deep you feel in bondage or how long you have been there. You will not need to live with the feeling of inadequacy all of your life. Many rejected people feel like a constant failure. They feel like everything that they do or touch will fail, even their relationship with God. Often they feel inferior to other believers and wonder why they do not have the same intimacy with God that others have.
   *Where was God?*

---

[5] Inner Healing – Dunklin Memorial Ministries – used by permission.

God is sovereign. He rules this universe with an unmatched intelligence while at the same time not violating His original purpose for man. He wants a love relationship with man. However, in order to enjoy a love relationship, man must have the potential for the opposite, which is a rejection of His sovereign rule and His love. Without your free volition, you could not truly love. Therefore, evil people do evil things. That is why so many things happen in our lives for which we have no explanation. You might ask, "Where was God when my father rejected me?" Or, "Where was God when my close relative raped me at an early age?" "I had no choice in those matters." One could ask why God allowed Job, a "perfect man," to go through what he endured. By the way, we have a booklet on that subject titled Job's Journey.[6]

No one can give you an adequate answer to those "why" questions except for the fact that we live in a sin filled world. However, I believe that the Word of God gives us some answers that can bring us peace, security, closure, and purpose. Jesus' work on the Cross and His resurrection, coupled with your new birth resulting from that work, gives you the potential, through grace, to convert every tragic experience in your life into a blessing. I believe that the more tragic the experience, the larger the potential blessing. I could not be doing the work that God has me doing in the Kingdom of God had it not been for my tragic past experiences. I know that Michael and Karen are being greatly used by God in bringing inner healing programs to scores of people in many nations only because of their tragic past. Rather than despising your past, allow God to convert your "junk" into "jewels," as defined in our book, Junk to Jewels. [7]

## God's priorities and purposes.

In addition, I think it is important to keep in mind God's priorities and purposes. I do not believe that it is God's purpose to give us an easy life, making sure that we do not suffer in any way. While

---

[6] http://www.isob-bible.org/lc-upload/job/job.pdf
[7] http://www.isob-bible.org/biblepick.htm

## Chapter 4 – Wounds From Others

He does not dispense suffering, it is a means that He uses to carry out one of His primary purposes, that being the defeat of Satan and his band of followers in finality. Job's experience defeated the satanic power in Job's realm of influence. I believe that is the primary theme of the Book of Job. Paul's "messenger from Satan," his "thorn in the flesh," (2 Corinthians 12) was defeated in Paul's life. Overcoming wounds and circumstances that produce suffering is about more than giving us freedom, it is also about defeating those satanic beings and curses that are in our realm of influence.

"I now rejoice in my sufferings for you, and fill up in my flesh what is lacking in the afflictions of Christ, for the sake of His body, which is the church" (Colossians 1:24).

We need to be reminded that the way that God manifests His priorities and primary purposes in our lives is through the fruit bearing process. God works by seed, time and harvest. His Word is the seed that goes into our hearts to produce His will for our lives and for the Kingdom of God. This is all covered in Mark chapter 4, and in detail in our book Grow or Die [8]. Notice however in Mark chapter 4 that not all the types of people bear fruit, and that Satan is at work to destroy the seed and prevent the fruit.

The reason I am bringing this up in this book and chapter is that with too many inner unhealed wounds we are not good candidates for bearing fruit. We need to take this healing process seriously because it affects our eternal purpose.

## The most powerful positive force in the universe is the love of God.

God is love; therefore, love is God's most powerful force. We were created for there to be with a deep connection between God and us. Psalm 139:13-16 says, "For You formed my inward parts; You covered me in my mother's womb. I will praise You, for I am fearfully *and* wonderfully made; Marvelous are Your works, And

---

[8] Web link for Grow or Die book. http://www.isob-bible.org/component/content/article.html?id=292

## Chapter 4 – Wounds From Others

*that* my soul knows very well. My frame was not hidden from You, When I was made in secret, *And* skillfully wrought in the lowest parts of the earth. Your eyes saw my substance, being yet unformed. And in Your book they all were written, The days fashioned for me, When *as yet there were* none of them."

Ephesians 1:4-5 says, "just as He chose us in Him before the foundation of the world, that we should be holy and without blame before Him in love, having predestined us to adoption as sons by Jesus Christ to Himself, according to the good pleasure of His will."

We were also formed connected to our mothers. These bridges were built for love, acceptance, and were to travel between the three, God, mother, and child. It is an emotional and even physical need; we need love and acceptance just as much as food and water. God created us with these needs because He has what it takes to fulfill these needs through a relationship with Him.

1 John 4:8,16 (NASB) says, "The one who does not love does not know God, for God is love." "We have come to know and have believed the love, which God has for us. God is love and the one who abides in love abides in God, and God abides in him."

**Rejection is the opposite of the love of God.**
If love is the most powerful positive force in creation, it follows that lack of love is the most powerful negative force in creation. Rejection is the denial of love and acceptance in our lives. A connection is broken when there is a lack of touch, verbal communication and the feeling of security.

Often our bridges become broken or damaged through rejection. Rejection is probably the most painful, the most neglected; yet one of the most common emotional wounds from which we suffer. These broken relationships and rejection issues come in all sizes and shapes and from so many different sources. Later in this chapter we will look at wounds caused in a marriage. Even at wounds caused by a church, church family or church authority figure can be damaging.

Some of the forms of rejection are denial, refusal, and rebuff, slighting, shunning, spurning, ignoring, neglecting, avoiding, and disapproving. It becomes obvious that rejection is not always physical. Nor is it always recognizable.

***Rejection can lead to fear of further rejection and self-rejection.*** Some of the manifestations of the fear of rejection, according to the Inner Healing book we have been using are, anger, bitterness, cults and gangs, self-rejection, hurt, self-pity, despair, depression, isolation and suicide.

**Rejection really hurts, finds brain study.**
Source: New Scientist - Date: 9 October 2003

*Lonely hearts have spent millennia trying to capture the pain of rejection in painting, poetry and song. Now neuroscientists have seen it flickering in some remarkable brain images from college students suffering a social snub.*

*The brain scans reveal that two of the same brain regions that are activated by physical pain are also activated by social exclusion.*

I interviewed a lady who has been a social worker in nursing homes for quite some time and has studied Alzheimer's and dementia at great lengths. She informed me that when a person has a traumatic event it causes an excess of adrenaline to pump into the brain. The result is that a "chemical marker" is placed on the brain. This marker has the potential to replay the traumatic event over and over. This lady is a Christian. I asked if she thought that inner healing and forgiveness through the Blood of Jesus could heal this issue. She said definitely yes. I submit that the marker changes from a scab to a scar. We will cover this issue in a later chapter. Former addicts tell us that they have experienced a "euphoric recall" from these markers, which are sometimes caused by music that they listened to, drugs, pornography, or other thrill causing events. Veterans from wars often suffer from the trauma they saw.

***One of the by-products of rejection is a broken spirit.***

## Chapter 4 – Wounds From Others

Proverbs 15:13 (NASB) says, "A joyful heart makes a cheerful face, but when the heart is sad, the spirit is broken.

***A broken spirit, brought about by rejection is capable of "drying up," or taking away the desire for life.***

Proverbs 17:22 (NASB) says, "A joyful heart is good medicine, but a broken spirit dries up the bones."

***If the desire for life has gone, there is no chance for healing to take place.***

Proverbs 18:14 (NASB) says, "The spirit of a man can endure his sickness, but as for a broken spirit who can bear it?"

**Some fruits of rejection.**

***The Inner Healing book we are using lists in Session Four the following issues having to do with the fruit of rejection.***

Rejection acts like a tree with a bitter root. It can only produce bitter fruit. The growth and fruit will vary with the degree of rejection. Listed below are some examples of the fruit rejection produces:

- Inability to receive love - we believe we are unworthy.
- Inability to love others - we stay at a distance, not trusting.
- Insecurity - we expect to be rejected.
- Withdrawal - safety in isolation.
- Suspicion - everybody is out to get us.
- Inferiority - because we feel unworthy.
- Social shyness - everyone else is superior.
- Fear of failure - confirms my belief that I am a failure.
- Fear of man - "if they only knew who I was..."
- Fear of rejection - keeps us from being ourselves.
- Self-rejection - we actually believe the lies to be true.
- Daydreaming/fantasizing - we create our own reality.

*How rejection wounds us.*

God created us to be in relationship with Him as our loving Father. Bad earthly relationships create wounds in our inner being that we don't even recognize as wounds. These wounds not only cause us to live ungodly lifestyles, but they also keep us from a relationship with God our Father and Jesus.

The solution is simple to describe but not so simple to walk through. First we have to allow the Holy Spirit to lead us in the discipline of discovering the deep roots that have power in our lives. Then we bring them to Jesus and His Cross. We forgive those who wounded us, and we receive forgiveness from God and others who we have offended. And then we are to pursue with all of our hearts a close, intimate and conversational relationship with Jesus and our Father God. We will then discover the truth that Jesus bore our wounds at the Cross on our behalf. Really believing that truth will set you free!

**Isaiah 53:4-5 says,**

*"4 Surely He has borne our griefs And carried our sorrows; Yet we esteemed Him stricken, Smitten by God, and afflicted.*

*"5 But He was wounded for our transgressions, He was bruised for our iniquities; The chastisement for our peace was upon Him, And by His stripes we are healed."*

As we showed in a previous chapter, Jesus performed a miracle as recorded in Mark chapter 2. This story of the paralytic shows us that forgiveness, i.e., the sin of rejection borne by Jesus instead of you, brings inner healing. With this inner healing the fruits and manifestations produced by rejection eventually go away.

**You may not be paralyzed in body, but maybe in spirit or in lifestyle.**

Maybe you are too paralyzed to stop using drugs. Maybe you are eating to medicate your relationship emptiness; maybe you are doing destructive things to your body like cutting or other such painful acts. Maybe you cannot stop inordinate sex, looking at pornography, anger, or depression. It could be simply being extremely performance oriented or self-righteous in order to cover the pain. Some use adventure, overindulging in sports and other

## Chapter 4 – Wounds From Others

daredevil activities, and the list goes on. Your external paralysis has an inner cure for which Jesus paid the ultimate price. Perhaps you are just not experiencing the "abundant life."

**Other types of wounds, rejection from others. The following is a quote from Dunklin.** [9]

*Many people come from dysfunctional homes. That doesn't necessarily mean alcoholism or drug abuse is in the home. Alcohol and drug abuse are merely forms of dysfunction. There are many forms of dysfunction, but to simplify the term, any home in which Christ is not the Head, is dysfunctional.*

*Physical abuse, mental abuse, sexual abuse, or even a highly demanding parent can produce dysfunction in a home. The parent who requires constant perfection initiates a climate of performance orientation in the home. The child is prompted to perform to receive love and attention. This is a dysfunctional home atmosphere!*

**Physical abuse.**

*The physically abused child is immediately filled with fear and confusion. There is no doubt in its mind that it has been rejected. Deep down, feelings of anger, and a desire to get even and to punish, begin to build. Because the child has an abusive role model, he is likely to become an abuser, himself.*

**Sexual abuse.**

*The child who has been subject to molestation develops an inability to be open and warm with people. He usually displays a victim mentality, and lacks the ability to trust anyone, especially authority figures.*

*The wounds from sexual abuse run deep. They have caused many people to live lifestyles that are very*

---

[9] Inner Healing Copyright 1992 by Dunklin Memorial Church – Used by permission ISOB.
Web link: http://www.isob-bible.org/openlessons.htm#heal

*destructive. They seem to cause despair and hopelessness. I have seen lives that have been marvelously healed and that are being greatly used by God for the healing of others.*

***Rejection and inner wounds from a broken marriage relationship.***

While wounds received during our youthful years can be more damaging, wounds received in a less than perfect marriage, both on us and our children, can be very damaging and are candidates for inner healing. The Holy Spirit's ministry is to bring forgiveness, repentance, correction and consequently healing.

The marriage is a blood covenant, which like all blood covenants requires the death of both parties to serve one another. Anything short of this produces wounds that need healing both in the marriage partners and in the children. Jeremiah 34:18-20 states that the covenant breaker will be given into the hands of his/her enemies. However, we know that forgiveness and repentance will take the enemy off of our lives.

The commitment in marriage is far greater than saying, "I will never get a divorce." Making that statement and then spending more time with your friends than you do with your spouse will make your marriage a living divorce! The commitment is about what you *will do*, not so much what you *will not do*.

Having said all of that, God desires to cleanse you from any condemnation of a broken marriage. If you played a part in the problem, and you repent, you are forgiven; your sins are totally eradicated. If your former or current spouse has sinned against you, you must practice forgiveness in order to be free.

Some doctrines regarding divorce being the unpardonable sin are pure heresy, and perpetrate constant condemnation of people that they cannot overcome.

God never intended to infer that in the Word of God. We have a series called "Healing From The Wounds of Marriage" which is available at our website, http://www.isob-bible.org/marriage/tocmar.htm. Another great resource is a book written by Dr. M.G. McLuhan, Marriage and Divorce. [10] Dr. McLuhan was associate pastor of Mount Paran Church of God in Atlanta Georgia during its greatest time of growth. He personally helped my wife and I very much, as did Dr. Paul L. Walker, the senior pastor.

**When wounded people attack you.**
There will be time when a wounded person attacks you as a result of the wound that resides in them. It may be a family member or church member or just anybody you may encounter.

When this has happened to me I used to feel resentment. However the Lord Jesus has changed me, and now, most of the time, I feel mercy! This person usually has no idea that they are hurting you as it is usually subconscious.

*Forgive.*
First you must forgive that person and ask God to forgive the resentment or anger you may have. If you sense the anointing, bind that trait that has attacked you, perhaps jealousy, anger or many others. I have seen healing take place as you have utilized the anointing in the binding and loosing authority that Jesus gives. As we understand what is already bound or loosed in Heaven, we have the authority and responsibility to bring God's order and healing to it. The supernatural takes place and healing takes place.

*What Jesus said about binding and loosing. It was a key aspect of our part of the Kingdom of God.*
**Matthew 16:18-19 AMP says,**

*18 And I tell you, you are Peter [Greek, Petros —a large piece of rock], and on this rock [Greek, petra —a huge rock like Gibraltar] I will build My church, and the gates of Hades (the powers of the infernal region) shall not overpower it [or be strong to its detriment or hold out against it].*

---

[10] McLuhan, M.G.. Marriage And Divorce. Tyndale House Publishers. Wheaton IL. 1991.

## Chapter 4 – Wounds From Others

*19 I will give you the keys of the kingdom of heaven; and whatever you bind (declare to be improper and unlawful) on earth must be what is already bound in heaven; and whatever you loose (declare lawful) on earth must be what is already loosed in heaven.*

**God created us with a need for a father. Father rejection is one of the worst kind.**
From what I have learned, any break with our "father" relationship is the key to our feeling of rejection and inner wounds. As mentioned before, it may or may not be a *direct* father break. It could be a generational iniquity coming down from former generational fathers. It simply could be the break from the time of Adam and God.

***David stated it simply in Psalm 27.***
David acknowledged to God that his parents, brothers and family could have been far from perfect, but that his one desire was to be God's son and then to be in continual fellowship with His Heavenly Father.

Psalm 27:10 (Amplified Bible) says, "Although my father and my mother have forsaken me, yet the Lord will take me up [adopt me as His child]."

Psalm 27:4 (Amplified Bible) says, "One thing have I asked of the Lord, that will I seek, inquire for, and [insistently] require: that I may dwell in the house of the Lord [in His presence] all the days of my life, to behold and gaze upon the beauty [the sweet attractiveness and the delightful loveliness] of the Lord and to meditate, consider, and inquire in His temple."

Jesus did not pay the price for our forgiveness and healing just to go about our lives in the same old way. He paid the most expensive price so that we, like David, would be in constant fellowship with our Father.

Chapter 4 – Wounds From Others

**In his book [11] <u>God A Good Father</u>, author Michael Phillips makes some profound statements about the fatherhood of God that have really fastened themselves upon my soul.**

*The most important truth in all the universe can be stated in four words: God is our Father. To the extent we apprehend God's Fatherhood will our life be integrated, whole, and complete in relationship to the Creator, who made us to live in the surroundings in which he has placed us.*

*When we read the Gospels with our newly trained eyes, we begin to see that God's Fatherhood is the single truth toward which Jesus always points. It was the entire focal point of His mission on earth.*

*In this mission, however, Jesus forged new ground. Aside from a few instances, throughout the Old Testament God had not been perceived as a Father. There was no doctrine of the Trinity – no concept of Father, no knowledge of Son, no awareness of Holy Spirit. Yahweh was "one." Father was arguably the last term anyone would have used to describe Him.*

*Nor was the Jew's religion in Jesus' day a personal one. They viewed God primarily as Lawgiver and Judge. Moses and David walked in intimate friendship with God, but not so the masses. The Law was to be obeyed, and the Almighty Judge called Yahweh stood ready to render judgment when it was broken.*

*Nowhere in the theological or philosophical world of Jesus' time, then, was divine character equated with Fatherhood.*

*Earthly fathers have dulled the magnificence of God's Fatherhood almost beyond recognition. His Fatherhood is the essential human instinct; that created yearning to look up and behold our Father"* (Paraphrased by author).

---

[11] God A Good Father, Michael Phillips, Destiny Image Publishers, Inc., Shippensburg, PA., 2001, Pages 43-49

## Chapter 4 – Wounds From Others

**Jesus came to heal and to save mankind from the broken father relationship.**
I noticed in the Old Testament that often God had prompted people to leave their father's house and follow Him. There is overwhelming evidence of the corrupt fatherhood by most men throughout the Old Testament; fathers who did not perform their proper father functions of discipline, love, care, affirmation, morality, fidelity, etc.

A look and study into John chapter 8 will show Jesus' heart about this issue. While the Jews at one point stated that Abraham was their father, when Jesus challenged them they even said that God was their father. Jesus quickly informed them that actually the Devil was their father. He informed them that sin in their lives must first be dealt with in order for God to be their Father.

Most of Jesus' last words to his disciples as recorded in John chapters 14-17 had to do with reconnecting us to the Father. He spoke of the Holy Spirit coming to be our connector to Father God. Jesus is the way, meaning to prepare things and referring to the Word, but the Holy Spirit is the person who really makes the connection real-time

*God breathed.*
God the Father breathed into Adam, and became Adam's father, Genesis 2:7. Jesus breathed into the disciples on behalf of the Father God and again God became our Father, John 20:22. This is how we were born again and now can enjoy belonging to a new Father and race of people.

*Jesus is the way to the Father.*
In order to have continual fellowship and oneness with our Father God we need Jesus. The Word is Jesus, therefore the Word is the way to the Father. "Jesus said to him, "I am the way, the truth, and the life. No one comes to the Father except through Me" (John 14:6).

*Jesus revealed the tenderness of the Father.*
"Jesus said to him, 'Have I been with you so long, and yet you have not known Me, Philip? He who has seen Me has seen the

## Chapter 4 – Wounds From Others

Father; so how can you say, 'Show us the Father'?" (John 14:9). If the Father is like Jesus, then we can say "Abba," Daddy, with confidence. Galatians 4:6 says, "And because you are sons [huios [12]], God has sent forth the Spirit of His Son into your hearts, crying out, 'Abba, Father!'"

John 16:27 (Amplified Bible) says, "For the Father Himself [tenderly] loves you because you have loved Me and have believed that I came out from the Father." Meditate and repeat this verse! "The Father tenderly loves me!" Go ahead say it!

***We have intimacy, oneness, with Jesus and the Father.***

"that they all may be one, as You, Father, are in Me, and I in You; that they also may be one in Us, that the world may believe that You sent Me" (John 17:21).

***This Father will never leave you!***

"For He Himself has said, 'I will never leave you nor forsake you'" (Hebrews 13:5b). You never have to fear again. Your conduct will not be perfect; you will still sin from time to time. Even then, your Father will never leave you nor forsake you. He will always be there to turn you around and bring you back. He is passionate about you.

**Put a picture in your mind and heart about God's love for you and how the sacrifice of Jesus on the Cross purchased your wholeness.**

Imagine a picture of Jesus standing between you and the person who abused you, actually bearing the abuse for you. Imagine that the abuse could not actually affect you because Jesus absorbed it. This is really where Jesus was when you were rejected and abused.

---

[12] Huios defined in Strong's Concordance: those who revere God as their father, those who in character and life resemble God, those who are governed by the Spirit of God, repose the same calm and joyful trust in God which children do in their parents (Rom. 8:14, Gal. 3:26), and hereafter in the blessedness and glory of the life eternal will openly wear this dignity of the sons of God. Term used preeminently of Jesus Christ, as enjoying the supreme love of God, united to him in affectionate intimacy, privy to his saving councils, obedient to the Father's will in all his acts.

## Chapter 4 – Wounds From Others

He was right there, taking and bearing the sin on your behalf. Also keep that in your mind when you sin against others. If you allow Jesus to absorb the sin by forgiving the person who abused you, you will be set free! If you do not accept that truth and chose not to forgive, you will continue to be a victim, and will remain a bruised person.

"Surely He has borne our griefs And carried our sorrows; Yet we esteemed Him stricken, Smitten by God, and afflicted. But He *was* wounded for our transgressions, *He was* bruised for our iniquities; The chastisement for our peace *was* upon Him, And by His stripes we are healed" (Isaiah 53:4-5).

## We can have confidence in having a Father who cares for us and our every need.

"And in that day you will ask Me nothing. Most assuredly, I say to you, whatever you ask the Father in My name He will give you" (John 16:23). I believe I could paraphrase this as follows: "In that day, after my resurrection and when you have the Holy Spirit, you may approach the Father as I approach Him because you will have the same "name" or character that I have. He will treat you just as He treats Me. He will take care of your every need (even the discipline that you need to conform to My name)."

## The solution.

If most of our inner wounds come from rejection, and the worst rejection or broken relationship is with that of a father, then the ultimate connection that heals is with our Father God. Rejection is the most powerful negative force, while love is the most powerful positive force.

*Therefore inner healing has two primary steps.*

1. Seeing Jesus as our sin bearer, thus being able to forgive those who rejected us and to repent for the sin that these rejections caused us to make. This is the door to the next step.

2. Being in fellowship with our Father through our continual transparency and through Jesus the Word, and building that relationship with Him by obedience and mutual interchange. We

## Chapter 4 – Wounds From Others

must "take up our cross," as it stated all through the New Testament and as described in Romans 12:1-2 which says,

*"I beseech you therefore, brethren, by the mercies of God, that you present your bodies a living sacrifice, holy, acceptable to God, which is your reasonable service.*

*And do not be conformed to this world, but be transformed by the renewing of your mind, that you may prove what is that good and acceptable and perfect will of God."*

**Jesus was rejected and wounded for you.**
I pray that the Holy Spirit makes these Scriptures real to you.

"And at the ninth hour Jesus cried out with a loud voice, saying, "Eloi, Eloi, lama sabachthani?" which is translated, 'My God, My God, why have You forsaken Me?'" (Mark 15:34).

"He is despised and rejected by men, A Man of sorrows and acquainted with grief. And we hid, as it were, *our* faces from Him; He was despised, and we did not esteem Him" (Isaiah 53:3).

**Rejection exercise:**
First, ask God in prayer to reveal to you five rejections you experienced before the age of ten. Then ask Him to show you what bitter roots you have because of each rejection suffered and what fruit you have in your life because of these roots.

To pray through these incidences ask God to show you where He was when this deep-rooted rejection occurred. Ask God to show you the anger and resentment you had towards Him, yourself and others because of these rejections and repent.

# Chapter 5
# Wounds From Generational Curses

As I have studied cultures around the world, it became clear that most cultures have a default religion often called animism. Among that word's definitions is the worship of ancestral spirits, our forefathers who have passed away. I have seen food bowls sitting on top of graves so that the spirits can have something from which to eat. The interesting thing is that these bowls have holes drilled into them in order to keep them unusable by humans thus keeping them from being taken.

Sometimes this worship is intentional which is usually manifested in more primitive cultures. They actually carry out worship rituals, and feel that certain ancestors are responsible for certain types of blessings in their lives. Often in more civilized cultures, I believe that animism is more subconscious and not so intentional. It is propagated in different ways thus giving a powerful path on which generational curses may travel. Often, but not in all cases, family reunions can be a powerful tool that demons can use. Festivals in many cultures are similar to family reunions. They celebrate that passing year and vow to keep the demonic and family worship going for another year. We have seen this in Haiti first hand. I believe that Mardi Gras in New Orleans, Louisiana, is a "child" of this Haitian tradition. In my opinion, these festivals are counterfeits of God's festivals that were meant to pass on His blessings.

However, it is propagated, it is idol worship. Idol worship is demon worship and is powerful in the spiritual world.

Most idols going back into the history of the Old Testament days had some sort of perverted sexual connotation. Satan's tactics in this area are very cunning. He knows how easily a person can become entangled in idolatry and satanic influence through perverted sex.

**Who is your family?**
Jesus spoke often about "hating" your family in preference to God. Obviously, He did not use "hate" as we often define it. He meant

## Chapter 5 – Wounds From Generational Curses

that we must not put the natural family in first place, but rather be translated into the new family of the Kingdom of God. He knew that family control often kept people from making a 100% commitment to God. Matthew 12:50 says, "For whoever does the will of My Father in heaven is My brother and sister and mother."

People spend hours of time and thousand of dollars in an effort to track their generational linage and family trees. There is nothing wrong with that and it can even be helpful and valuable. I know many people who are fourth and fifth generation ministers in a powerful Spirit-filled denomination who have received a valuable legacy, a blessing from their forefathers. However, the best linage to trace and the best family tree to focus on is the one that was the result of your second birth, not your first natural birth.

When you make a firm commitment to make Jesus the Lord over every single aspect of your life, He will reveal to you that you are a New Creation, a member of a new race that Jesus started when He was raised from the dead. He was the first-born; your number is in there somewhere.

I submit that once you see, really see, who you really are, that you will begin to conform your outer life to who you are inside. It is time to stop being critical of yourself, despising your habits and failures, and take the step towards discovering the truth, that Christ is in you, the hope of glory. As you begin to see the truth, you will be *Free To Be You.*

### Adam.

Adam, the original man, was created to be normal. That meant he had God's Spirit abiding in him. He was told to stay connected with God through the Word, the Tree of Life, and not to trust in his independent intellect. As he did indeed begin to trust in his independence from God's Word, he found himself a prisoner to Satan, and he and all of his descendants experienced the trauma of being disconnected from God.

As we have studied, we were all born with this disconnection and we were free to make a choice to be redeemed with a new and second birth. As we made that choice, however, we found

## Chapter 5 – Wounds From Generational Curses

ourselves with old thoughts about our identity. The Bible tells us that we need to have our mind renewed so that we can see the truth of what really happened at our new birth. Actually, it is so awesome that we have a difficult time believing. Some of the difficulty has to do with Satan's deception, the deception of the culture, the world system, and our own "stinking thinking."

**Blessings and curses.**
*Jesus bore all your curses!*
As you read through this chapter you will see that Jesus actually bore all of your curses, generational, the ones caused by your own sin, all of them! Our overcoming involves overcoming the demonic forces that try to paste the curses back on us, not overcoming the curses, which have been borne by the Blood of Jesus.

**Revelation 12:11 says,**
*"11 "And they overcame him* **[Notice we overcome him, Satan, not the curse]** *by the blood of the Lamb and by the word of their testimony, and they did not love their lives to the death."*

God established the earth and mankind to be blessed. The first words He spoke to Adam was about a blessing. "So God created man in His *own* image; in the image of God He created him; male and female He created them. Then God blessed them, and God said to them, 'Be fruitful and multiply; fill the earth and subdue it; have dominion over the fish of the sea, over the birds of the air, and over every living thing that moves on the earth'" (Genesis 1:27-28).

However, there always must be a potential opposite for everything with God. If there is love then there must be the potential for hate. If there is obedience there must be the potential for disobedience, or sin. Therefore, if there are to be blessings, there must also be the potential for curses. This has been called a *"dysfunctional necessity."*

**Blessings for obedience, curses for disobedience.**

## Chapter 5 – Wounds From Generational Curses

A curse is the opposite of a blessing. A blessing is some type of prosperity that is the result of good and positive words or deeds. A curse is some type of failure caused or propagated by wicked or negative words or deeds. In Deuteronomy 28 and 29 Moses lists the blessings if one obeys the commandments of God and the curses if one does not obey the commandments of God.

I believe that a major theme of the Bible is turning curses into blessings. The curse was pronounced in Genesis, and the end of the curse is in Revelation. I also believe that often the process of removing curses is "overcoming."

### Exodus 34:5-8 says that curses are passed down to future generations.

"Keeping mercy for thousands, forgiving iniquity and transgression and sin, by no means clearing *the guilty*, visiting the iniquity of the fathers upon the children and the children's children to the third and the fourth generation" (Exodus 34:7).

God's original purpose was for us to have blessings passed down to future generations, which would have resulted from man's free will in right relationship to Him. However, justice demands that if blessings can be passed down so must curses be passed down.

There is an apparent paradox in what God told Moses in Exodus 34:5-8. He said that He would forgive, yet still pass down the iniquity to future generations.

*How could He do both? Good question.* God's justice cannot just overlook iniquity and sin. Therefore He did pass it down to future generations and it eventually went on Jesus, the perfect Lamb who bore it for all of us. He became a curse for us, Galatians 3:13.

*Curses and blessings are subject to the law of sowing and reaping.* If your grandfather sowed the sin of anger and rage, you and/or your children may be in line for far more anger and rage than your grandfather ever committed. He sowed the seed, however, the fruit is always more abundant than the seed. If you do a little drinking of alcohol, don't be surprised if your children or grandchildren are plagued with substance addictions including substances more dangerous than alcohol. We have overcome physical infirmities that have been experienced by our ancestors. While we have no idea how these originated, we do know that they were passed down. However, with our overcoming we know that our children and their children will never have to suffer with these issues. That "generation has passed away" (Matthew 24:34).

When Jesus said, "Assuredly, I say to you, this generation will by no means pass away till all these things take place" (Matthew 24:34), I believe He was not only talking about the end of the world, but He also was referring to the generational curse in your individual life. In Matthew 24 He was talking about all kinds of tragedies taking place as a prelude to the curse being overcome. That process is overcoming.

**Despair and hopelessness?**
*In his book titled **Blessing or Curse** [13] Derek Prince defines some of the affects of a curse.*
*...You, too, may have tasted success. You do indeed know the sweetness of it-but it never lasts! Suddenly, for no reason you can explain, you are dissatisfied. Depression settles over you like a cloud. All your achievements seem so insubstantial. You look at others who appear content in similar circumstances, and you ask yourself, "What's wrong with me? Why don't I ever experience real fulfillment?"*

**"*Wrestling against shadows*" is one of the phrases Derek Prince uses.**
In my life, when I experienced the affects of a curse, whether it was a product of my own doing or something that was passed down through the generations, my self-esteem level was at zero. I was made to feel like there was something terribly wrong with me,

---

[13] Prince, Derek. *Blessing or Curse*. Grand Rapids, MI: Chosen Books, 1990

## Chapter 5 – Wounds From Generational Curses

and I experienced great despair and hopelessness. This was during a time when I had a very intense relationship with the Lord.

People can react to this in different ways. Some just sink down under the weight of despair and give up, others become performance-oriented and seek to establish their own self-esteem based upon their works. I never gave up but rather gained relief on a daily basis by fellowshipping with the Lord in His Word. I can remember the Lord teaching me during that time about curses and blessings, and about myself. Eventually God gave me my self-esteem based upon having my identity in Him. Looking back, I think that the inner healing came before the actual curse was overcome and before circumstances started looking brighter. I entreat you now to be honest with God. Let Him know if there are areas in your life like this. It will be the beginning of your freedom. The truth will always make you free!

**Jesus encountered several people who were bound with infirmities and/or demons that apparently were generational in nature.**
In Mark chapter 9:17-29, Jesus cast a demon out of a young man who had been demon possessed from his childhood. The disciples could not cast out this demon, and after Jesus did the job they asked Him about it. "So He said to them, 'This kind can come out by nothing but prayer and fasting'" (Mark 9:29). Apparently, there were some issues that had to be dealt with besides the fact that a demon was present.

We need to see Jesus' heart in dealing with generational spiritual bondages. First, He wants us free. Next, He is sovereign and often takes the initiative. Also, He heals us without condemnation. I am not saying that we will not be uncomfortable, or that God will not confront us with some tough issues and tough disciplines, but He does not condemn. The Holy Spirit does convict, and we need to be mature and honest enough to allow Him to do so.

In John chapter 9, Jesus was walking with His disciples and He noticed a man blind from his birth. How did He know the man

## Chapter 5 – Wounds From Generational Curses

was blind from birth? Who knows? Perhaps it was a word of knowledge; maybe God had spoken to Him in prayer the night before. This man was not seeking to be healed; Jesus sought him out of a crowd.

John 9:2 says, "And His disciples asked Him, saying, 'Rabbi, who sinned, this man or his parents, that he was born blind?'" They thought that infirmities were due to sin, perhaps the sin of the parents, perhaps a deeper generational curse just as Moses had discovered. Jesus answered the question in a way that I believe the Amplified version states the best. "Jesus answered, 'It was not that this man or his parents sinned, but he was born blind in order that the workings of God should be manifested (displayed and illustrated) in him.'" (John 9:3, Amplified Bible).

Obviously, all have sinned, including this man and his parents. The point was, that Jesus saw a higher purpose in the infirmity and knew that focusing on whose sin caused it would not be merciful, nor would it produce a cure. I believe Jesus was teaching that our "junk," viewed from God's perspective, was nothing more than raw material for "jewels."

So it is with our generational curses. I believe that Jesus has fasted and prayed, and that He comes to us with His power and He converts our curses to blessings. What I want to impart here is first, the knowledge of the subject, and second, how we can cooperate with God's effort to free us.

**Your purpose in life may never be realized if curses are not dealt with.**

Many years ago I was taking an extended walk with the Lord. In a moment of feeling that I wanted to totally consecrate myself to Him I said, "Lord, write your purpose on the tablet of my heart by the pen of the Word dipped into the ink of Holy Spirit." I just wanted whatever God wanted for my life, no more, no less.

I could see some sort of canvas inside of me with the Lord writing His plan on it for my life. "Keep my commands and live, and my law as the apple of your eye. Bind them on your fingers; Write them on the tablet of your heart" (Proverbs 7:2-3).

## Chapter 5 – Wounds From Generational Curses

The Lord responded, "I don't have to write; the plan for your life was written on your heart before the foundation of the world. The counterfeiter has stolen your canvas and has painted his plan on it, covering up My plan. What needs to be done now is to scrape away the counterfeit paint."

The Lord knew that I had met an artist one time that would steal beautiful paintings from galleries, not for their art beauty, but just for the value of the canvas. He would then paint his work over the original. This is the picture I saw.

I believe that God has a beautiful purpose for you, here on earth, one that will satisfy you beyond your greatest dreams, dreams that you may have never dreamed, but that are locked up inside of you (Ephesians 3:20).

I also believe that much of the counterfeit paint consists of old sin and especially generational curses, including things that happened to you when you were young, and things that happened to your forefathers before you were born. I can tell you two things from my experience. First, God has been taking me into my purpose and is still working it out. Second, it has not been easy; it has taken "overcoming" every step of the way. But nothing in life is easy, so why not go for the "gold."

***Abandonment is the requirement.***

Abandonment is believing and trusting. It is faith, and it really gets God's attention. If you do not live in total abandonment to God, most likely you will have many regrets when you see Jesus face to face. When you abandon yourself in faith to Jesus, you set Him free to accomplish His purpose for your life. You have to make room for Him or He will not operate. I believe that when God sees your abandonment, He will begin your journey to turn your curses into blessings.

**Here are some facts about generational curses extracted (in part) from the book <u>Blessing or Curse.</u>** [14]

---

[14] Prince, Derek. *Blessing or Curse*. Grand Rapids, MI:: Chosen Books, 1990

## Chapter 5 – Wounds From Generational Curses

1. The penalty for sin is the curse. The curse of eternal separation is the ultimate curse. If that has been settled, what about those of a lesser penalty? If He annulled death, He also annulled your curse.

2. A curse or a blessing is a supernatural power for good or for bad. Deuteronomy 28:21 says they cling, verse 29 says none can save.

3. Curses and blessings can be generational, passed down. They can be on families, nations, races, and regions.

4. Curses are usually propagated by words spoken, written or inward or by objects.

5. Curses are like a long arm from the past. Wrestling against shadows.

6. The primary cause of a curse is not hearing and obeying God, Deuteronomy 28.

*Some sources of curses.*

Deuteronomy 27:17 says that the person that who moves the boundaries is cursed. God gave us boundaries, and when we transgress them, we are cursed.

1. False Gods, Exodus 20:3-5.
2. Idolatry (occult), Deuteronomy 27:15.
3. Disrespect for parents, Proverbs 30:17.
4. Treachery…neighbor, Proverbs 17:13.
5. Injustice to the weak and poor, Proverbs 28:27.
6. Unnatural sex/incest, Leviticus 20:10-16.
7. Anti-Semitism, Genesis 12:3; 27:29.
8. Depending on the flesh, Jeremiah 17:5-7.
9. Stealing/perjury, Zechariah 5:1-4.
10. Stinginess, Malachi 3:8-10.
11. Perverting the true Gospel, Galatians 1:8-9.
12. Living by legalism, by the Law, and not by grace, Galatians 3:10.
13. Self-imposed (speaking negative words, and/or personal sin), Genesis 27:11-13; Matthew 27:24-25.
14. Servants of Satan, others cursing you like Balaam and Goliath, Numbers 22:6; 23:11-13; 1 Sam. 17:43.

## Chapter 5 – Wounds From Generational Curses

15. Deuteronomy 28:15 says that if we do not obey His commands, all these curses will come upon us. Most of the time we recognize our sin, and when we confess it we are cleansed. However, God commands us to "fear not." Fear, which is born out of an ignorance of God's great love for us, can bring curses. Fear can be the spirit connector to the curse.

### *Meeting the Conditions for breaking the curse.*

A curse cannot attach itself without a cause. "Like a flitting sparrow, like a flying swallow, so a curse without cause shall not alight" (Proverbs 26:2).

Jesus was the fulfillment of this promise. "Christ has redeemed us from the curse of the law, having become a curse for us (for it is written, 'Cursed *is* everyone who hangs on a tree')" (Galatians 3:13). Jesus bore every curse for every human being.

The way to make every curse have no cause is to cooperate in its transfer to Jesus, who bore it for us, and to hear and obey the Word of God. When we miss it, we confess our sin and we come back into right standing and obedience (1 John 1:9).

Even though Jesus bore our curse, demons have been assigned to attempt to propagate them on us, both believers and non-believers. They tempt us with thoughts, which tell us either that there is no such thing as a curse or that the Bible is not true regarding Jesus bearing our curse. They are able to cause us to sense the affects of the curse, which they hope will lead us to speak the curse into our lives rather than believe the Bible no matter what we feel. When we feel the affects of the curse, we are to remember that those affects are illegal, and that overcoming them will not only let us free, set others free, and also defeat those demons that have been active on us. We need to remember that this earth is subject to us now, even though Jesus defeated Satan at the Cross.

**Psalms 115:16 says,**
 *"16 The heaven, even the heavens, are the LORD'S; But the earth He has given to the children of men."*

### *Removal of the curse was a promise to Israel.*

Chapter 5 – Wounds From Generational Curses

We, the church, are reaping the benefits of the New Covenant ahead of time. Natural Israel will also enter into the New Covenant as told by Jeremiah. Jeremiah describes the promise in Jeremiah 31:29-34. However, verses 29-30 give a great picture that I urge you to keep in your mind and spirit. "In those days they shall say no more: 'The fathers have eaten sour grapes, And the children's teeth are set on edge.' But every one shall die for his own iniquity; every man who eats the sour grapes, his teeth shall be set on edge" (Jeremiah 31:29-30).

**Jesus took Barabbas' curse and yours as well.**
Matthew 27:16 says that Barabbas was a notorious prisoner. There were three crosses on Golgotha. The two on either side were made for criminals. Was the middle cross made for, Jesus? No, it was made for Barabbas. Jesus took his place. Isaiah 53 says that Jesus took our place.

Isaiah 53:4-6 says, "Surely He has borne our griefs and carried our sorrows; yet we esteemed Him stricken, smitten by God, and afflicted. But He was wounded for our transgressions, He was bruised for our iniquities; the chastisement of our peace was upon Him, and by His stripes we are healed. All we like sheep have gone astray; we have turned, every one, to his own way; and the LORD has laid on Him the iniquity of us all."

**The steps for becoming free from the affects of a curse are:**
1. Confess your faith in the finished work of the Cross, that Jesus took every curse that could come on you. Lift up Jesus, as the Israelites lifted up the snake on the brass pole (Numbers 21). Place the reaping of the consequences of sin, perhaps that of your forefathers or even your own, on the Cross.

2. Confess your faith that Jesus is the Son of God, the only way to God, and that He died on the Cross and rose again.

3. Repentance is a powerful way to deal with curses. Repent from all rebellion and sin, and submit to Jesus as Lord. This may include your personal repentance as well as corporate repentance for your family or whoever is affected by this curse. In the case of

## Chapter 5 – Wounds From Generational Curses

our children, we should repent for them, and for our forefathers who may have passed this curse down as well as for ourselves.

4. Forgiveness. Claim forgiveness for all of your sins, especially for the sins that exposed you to a curse. Forgive others who have wronged you or disappointed you.

***Look back at your forefathers' sins and forgive them. Then put the fruit of those sins on the Cross of Jesus who bore their fruit.*** After you ask God to forgive you, then look back as far as you can and ask God to forgive your forefathers for passing the curse down to you. Ask for release from consequences of your ancestor's sins.

***Following is a testimony from a friend of mine who has dealt with decades of drug addiction due to abuse from his father. A few years ago he really turned his life over to Jesus and was set free from the addictions, but there were still unresolved issues.***

***The resentment towards his now deceased father was so intense he found it nearly impossible to forgive him. He wrote the following to me:***

"I feel I received more inner healing today from the Holy Spirit regarding my father. A friend was talking to me after class regarding forgiving our fathers, and he said that unforgiveness towards our fathers can be generational, and that maybe my father had a lot of unforgiveness towards his father, and so on.

As soon as he said that I remembered a story my mother told years ago that I had completely forgotten about. When my father was a child, he came home from school one day and everything was gone. The house was empty, no furniture, no brothers, no sisters, no Mom, no Dad. They had moved away and didn't bother to tell him. They just flat out packed up and moved without saying a word to my Dad. I can't even imagine the feeling of fear and abandonment that my father felt at that moment in time as a child. As soon as the Holy Spirit brought that to my mind, I started crying, because of the love and compassion I felt for my Dad. I am crying now. I can't write any more.

## Chapter 5 – Wounds From Generational Curses

*Then this went into my heart so deep because I have been so self- centered with my focus on ME and how wounded I was and not taking into account how badly my father was wounded. When I realized this, the compassion and love for my father was so overwhelming I just started weeping and walked away from my friend to be alone in a corner of the classroom. I'm sure my friend was not offended.*

*I'm continually amazed at how the Holy Spirit speaks through other people in class to bring healing. It is truly amazing. The Holy Spirit set me free from the unforgiveness I've had towards my father for 49 years. 49 long years man. I have a humble, contrite, and grateful heart and I praise God Almighty for the healing.*
**Anonymous.**

After looking back, then look forward and ask God to forgive your children and pray to put the fruit of generational curses on Jesus instead of on them. Repentance in this manner is powerful. My wife and I can testify to that. We have seen supernatural blessings occur in this area.

5. Renounce all contact with anything occult or satanic, including objects that represent them.

6. Replace the void created with the Word of God. Ask God to give you the Word that will counteract the curse you have renounced. Then meditate upon it, memorize it, and continually confess it.

**Overcoming the affects of a curse may come immediately or it may take some time.**
Often it takes a period of time to become totally loosed from the affects of a curse. With some people it is immediate, with me it has more often required a lengthy process. I am not trying to bottle up God in a formula. He can work any way He wills. I am just giving you what my experience has been and how it has lined up with Scripture. We have seen victory and overcoming when we have lived out the overcoming lifestyle as I have explained. "And they overcame him by the blood of the Lamb and by the word of

## Chapter 5 – Wounds From Generational Curses

their testimony, and they did not love their lives to the death" (Revelation 12:11). We have also seen immediate manifestations of the path of healing and deliverance when we identified the problem and confessed our sin with repentance. Our job is to be honest and repent, God has the plan and the path customized for your life.

Very often in our lives, we have spent months and even years overcoming the curse, believing the Word of God no matter how our emotions were battering us. We have discovered that often overcoming curses over a lengthy period of time does more to defeat the satanic beings that have been propagating the curse, and sending them into their eternal defeat. Whatever the case, never give up! God knows what He is doing.

**Suggested prayers.**
*Scriptural basis*: "Lord Jesus Christ, I believe that on the cross you took every curse that could come on me."
*Faith in Christ:* "You are the Son of God, the only way to God; you died on the cross and rose again."
*Repentance:* "I give up all rebellion and sin, and I submit to you as Lord and Master."
*Claim forgiveness:* "I confess all my sins and ask your forgiveness, especially for sins that exposed me to a curse. Release me also from consequences of my ancestors' sins."
*Forgive:* "By a decision of my will, I forgive all who have wronged or disappointed me--just as I want God to forgive me."
*Renounce:* "I renounce all contact with anything occult or satanic. If I have "contact objects" I commit myself to destroy them. I cancel all Satan's claims against me." (See pp. 68-71 of Blessing or Curse: You Can Choose for list of occult practices. See pp. 121-124 of They Shall Expel Demons [15] for five signs of a cult.)
*Release*: "I ask you now to release me from every curse over my life. In your Name, Jesus, I release myself."

---

[15] Prince, Derek. *They Shall Expel Demons*. Grand Rapids, MI:: Chosen Books, 1998

Chapter 5 – Wounds From Generational Curses

**Now receive the exchange.**

| **Blessings** | **Curses** |
|---|---|
| Exaltation | Humiliation |
| Reproductiveness | Barrenness |
| Health | Sickness of all kinds |
| Prosperity | Poverty or failure |
| Victory | Defeat |
| Authority (head) | Helplessness (tail) |
| Above (strength) | Beneath (weakness) |

**Here is the point to remember. God's solution for us is to *see* and *believe*.**

There is a spiritual reality behind everything in the natural realm. The spiritual and invisible world is all around us but we cannot see it with our natural eyes. It is upholding everything that we can see with our eyes. Paul prayed in Ephesians chapter 1 that the people would have eyes to *see* the spiritual world. Ephesians 1:17-18 says, "that the God of our Lord Jesus Christ, the Father of glory, may give to you the spirit of wisdom and revelation in the knowledge of Him, the eyes of your understanding being enlightened; that you may know what is the hope of His calling, what are the riches of the glory of His inheritance in the saints." When we see the truth of the spiritual world, we will know the truth and we will be free, as Jesus said in John chapter 8.

Paul's prayer is that you and I may *see* the riches of the glory that is our inheritance. What is this glory? Colossians 1:27 says, "To them God willed to make known what are the riches of the glory of this mystery among the Gentiles: which is Christ in you, the hope of glory." The glory, the blessing, is Christ in you! You, the old person that is subject to curses, have been crucified with Christ (Galatians 2:20), however, the new man, Christ in you, is

## Chapter 5 – Wounds From Generational Curses

now living. And guess what, Christ in you cannot be subject to curses!

***We must see the good and the bad.***
First, you see the positive; that you were born again with the resurrected Christ who is now living in you, and who is not subject to being under a curse. Christ is not merely your example for living, He is not just somebody out there in Heaven helping you, but He has become your substitute, living His life in you instead of you living your old life.

God, in His mercy will help you to see yourself. As you stay close to God and spend time with Him in prayer and the Word, the Holy Spirit will convict you of strongholds, habits, and attitudes that are not Christlike. Use this reason: if Christ is living in me, then what is this in me that is not Christlike? This conviction is a gift of repentance from God. As you feel and sense bitterness, anger, jealousy, lust, etc., immediately bring it to Him as sin. Ask God to show you from where this originated. Open all of the doors of your heart and allow God to come into the closed areas of your life. Only He can heal them. Daniel was not harmed in the lion's den because, as the Scripture says, he was innocent with God. The Hebrew word for innocent is transparent - Daniel 6:21.

In years past, before I knew much at all about curses and blessings, God was releasing me from the affects of curses through my simple honesty and transparency with Him. I would continually look into the Word as a mirror and allow it to read me. Then I would confess all things in me that did not look like Jesus. This is really what you need to be free!

***The fact that curses are attempting to overtake you is based upon a lie!***
If Christ lives in you, then the issue of curses hurting you is legally settled. However, now you must possess that truth for yourself by seeing and believing. You must continue to see what is going on in the spiritual realm and affirming the truth of what you see. That is the only way to make it, because some curses don't just release the next day. Some demonic strongholds don't

## Chapter 5 – Wounds From Generational Curses

just go away like a scared dog. It may take patience and a lot of time affirming and testifying to the truth of the Cross. At the same time you must live a holy life, in other words, an honest life, so that your testimony is effective with God and with Satan. It may take some time for your mind to become renewed or the genetic factors to change, but as you continue to see and believe you are overcoming.

Seeing is your God-given heritage as a child of God. "But as it is written: 'Eye has not seen, nor ear heard, Nor have entered into the heart of man The things which God has prepared for those who love Him.' But God has revealed *them* to us through His Spirit. For the Spirit searches all things, yes, the deep things of God" (1 Corinthians 2:9-10).

**Remember our previous statements regarding curses.**
While the affects o curses are not desirable in our lives, they can be the raw material for "jewels" for the Kingdom of God. Remember the theme of the Book of Revelation. We saw Jesus at God's throne holding our Scroll with our curses recorded therein. After the process in Revelation, we see in its final chapters jewels making up God's Kingdom.

**On the Cross Jesus was cursed.**
But God spoke resurrection life into Him and He is now King! That same resurrection life spoken to you will also transform you and your life.

**When a generational curse is actually profitable! A lesson from Paul's thorn.**
The Apostle Paul repeatedly wrote that the weaknesses, trials and even sufferings that we experience is the primary thing that God uses to establish His Kingdom here on earth. It is not a popular message for many Christians, but it is truth, in Scripture, in our lives, and in the lives of many overcomers that we know personally.

## Chapter 5 – Wounds From Generational Curses

What Paul wrote in 2 Corinthians 3-4 goes along with his truth about this issue. He wrote in chapter 3 that the minds of the unbelievers are blinded, but that we have the light that they need. Then in chapter 4 he wrote that the light that they need which is in us needs to come out by our weaknesses, trials and even sufferings. I suggest that you read these chapters in their totality.

**2 Corinthians 4:7-12 says,**

*"7 But we have this treasure in earthen vessels, that the excellence of the power may be of God and not of us.*

*8 We are hard pressed on every side, yet not crushed; we are perplexed, but not in despair;*

*9 persecuted, but not forsaken; struck down, but not destroyed--*

*10 always carrying about in the body the dying of the Lord Jesus, that the life of Jesus also may be manifested in our body.*

*11 For we who live are always delivered to death for Jesus' sake, that the life of Jesus also may be manifested in our mortal flesh.*

*12 So then death is working in us, but life in you."*

For years I did not agree with many of the common theories about Paul's thorn in the flesh. One day suddenly the simplicity of the definition came to me. The word *thorn* in Scripture commonly refers to curse. What I write here is my opinion, and even if you disagree that should not take away from the main theme and idea of this chapter.

*Thorn:*
**Genesis 3:17-18 says,**

*"Then to Adam He said, "Because you have heeded the voice of your wife, and have eaten from the tree of which I commanded you, saying, 'You shall not eat of it': "Cursed is the ground for your sake; in toil you shall eat of it all the days of your life.*

## Chapter 5 – Wounds From Generational Curses

*Both thorns and thistles it shall bring forth for you, and you shall eat the herb of the field."*

### *Flesh:*

Paul commonly uses the word *flesh* as referring to our Adamic nature. Therefore I surmised that his thorn in the flesh was a curse that was chasing him, caused either by his own sin and/or by the sin of his forefathers. Paul had enough self-righteous religious activity in his life before meeting Jesus to bring that sin back on him.

### *Let's examine why Paul became so comfortable with his thorn in the flesh.*

First, I would like to review what Paul said in 2 Corinthians chapter 11 which I believe continues into chapter 12 wherein he talks about his thorn in the flesh. I believe that the sufferings he described in chapter 11 referred to his thorn.

When Paul was a Pharisee he sowed a lot of very bad seed by persecuting and even killing Jesus' followers. I believe that this caused a curse to attempt to come on him. It is also possible that Paul had ancestors from whom he inherited curses. However, Paul knew that he had been crucified with Christ, and that these curses had been borne by Jesus on the Cross for him. Therefore he determined to allow these attacks to work for the good of others through him. Paul discovered that the curses that were attempting to come upon him took him into the Heavenly Courtroom as a warrior where he could overcome and remove other people's blinders as a result. That, in my opinion, is why he did not despise them. Paul inherited this mindset from Jesus. In Gethsemane Jesus accepted the curse of all men, which led Him into the Heavenly Courtroom where He defeated Satan. Jesus wore a crown of thorns on the Cross, absorbing our curses.

**2 Corinthians 11:24-33 says,**

*"From the Jews five times I received forty stripes minus one.*

## Chapter 5 – Wounds From Generational Curses

*Three times I was beaten with rods; once I was stoned; three times I was shipwrecked; a night and a day I have been in the deep;*

*in journeys often, in perils of waters, in perils of robbers, in perils of my own countrymen, in perils of the Gentiles, in perils in the city, in perils in the wilderness, in perils in the sea, in perils among false brethren;*

*in weariness and toil, in sleeplessness often, in hunger and thirst, in fastings often, in cold and nakedness –*

*besides the other things, what comes upon me daily: my deep concern for all the churches.*

*Who is weak, and I am not weak? Who is made to stumble, and I do not burn with indignation?*

*If I must boast, I will boast in the things which concern my infirmity.*

*The God and Father of our Lord Jesus Christ, who is blessed forever, knows that I am not lying.*

*In Damascus the governor, under Aretas the king, was guarding the city of the Damascenes with a garrison, desiring to arrest me;*

*but I was let down in a basket through a window in the wall, and escaped from his hands."*

## 2 Corinthians 12:1-10 says,

*"7 And lest I should be exalted above measure by the abundance of the revelations, a thorn in the flesh was given to me, a messenger of Satan to buffet me, lest I be exalted above measure.*

*8 Concerning this thing I pleaded with the Lord three times that it might depart from me.*

*9 And He said to me, "My grace is sufficient for you, for My strength is made perfect in weakness." Therefore most gladly I will rather boast in my infirmities, that the power of Christ may rest upon me.*

## Chapter 5 – Wounds From Generational Curses

*10 Therefore I take pleasure in infirmities, in reproaches, in needs, in persecutions, in distresses, for Christ's sake. For when I am weak, then I am strong."*

Notice that the Lord did not tell Paul that His grace was insufficient, but that it was sufficient. God's grace, in my opinion, is Christ in you, performing and living out those things that no mere man can live out. I can tell you, that while I am overcoming the affects of generational curses in my own flesh, that I need to meditate on the benefits as spelled out by Paul in order to keep on going. Sometimes discouragement attacks like an arrow; bitterness and resentment swirl around my brain in an effort for me to welcome them. But in the end, no matter how I may feel, even while writing this now, I say with Paul, "Therefore I take pleasure in infirmities, in reproaches, in needs, in persecutions, in distresses, for Christ's sake. For when I am weak, then I am strong."

**Our cross is used like Jesus' was.**

In my experience, and by evidence of Scripture, as I go through the overcoming process, fighting the good fight of faith, not backing away from the wrestling match, God always brings good in the end. I have always seen many others blessed by what I went through and what I overcame. Jesus set this law in order from creation. Crucify a righteous man, and the perpetrator will be defeated. In the same way, try to perpetrate a curse, which may have been valid in the past, on a righteous follower of Jesus, and that perpetrator will also be defeated. And more than that, all of his other property or spoils will also be released. The Scripture says the following regarding setting others free through your overcoming.

**Luke 11:20-22 says,**

*"But if I cast out demons with the finger of God, surely the kingdom of God has come upon you.*

*When a strong man, fully armed, guards his own palace, his goods are in peace.*

*But when a stronger than he comes upon him and overcomes him, he takes from him all his armor in which he trusted, and divides his spoils."*

When we know for sure that all the enemies that attempt to torment us are already defeated, we can shout with joy as we see, in our mind's eye, the triumphant parade led by King Jesus with His enemies chained behind him as a public spectacle.

If you study the Book of Acts, you will notice that most of the time Paul was fruitful in his ministry right after he had suffered persecution and even physical beatings.

C. H. Spurgeon wrote,

*We must go to glory by the way of the weeping cross; and as we were never promised that we should ride to heaven in a feather bed, we must not be disappointed when we see the road to be rough, as our fathers found it before us.*

## Chapter 6
## Wounds From Our Own Sin

**Jesus wants to heal the wounds caused by our own sin.**
We will, in the next few chapters, deal with some specific common and strong personal sins that greatly affect us. Those are judgments, vows, and soul ties. In this chapter we will cover sin and rebellion in general. Whether it's the sin of judging others, making vows, soul ties, or just rebellion, your own sin will create a wound in your inner being, which only Jesus can heal, and that He longs to heal.

**First, I want to prepare you for what you are about to read.**
Acts 26:18 says, "to open their eyes, *in order* to turn *them* from darkness to light, and *from* the power of Satan to God, that they may receive forgiveness of sins and an inheritance among those who are sanctified by faith in Me."

We will be discussing sin. That can be good news or bad news. It all depends whether you are living in darkness or in the light. If you are in the light, then I submit you will have light to see the Good News, which includes:
1. Jesus.
2. The Word.
3. Yourself.
4. Your sin – by conviction not condemnation (Romans 8).
5. His love for you.
6. His forgiveness.
7. His grace.

***Light.***
If you are living in the light, then as my list above says, there is no condemnation. Even if you are struggling, you are living in the light, and you delight in God showing you what to repent for. You will be an overcomer if you stand. Do not accept the lies of the devil accusing you. The above list describes "walking in the Spirit" as indicated in Romans chapter 8:1.

## Chapter 6 – Wounds From Our Own Sin

*Darkness.*

If you are in darkness, then you will just feel condemnation, because as the Word says that there is probably some dark thing that you would rather not bring to the light. It may be that you are too embarrassed. It may be that you just enjoy your bad habit or area of sin so much that you don't want to give it up.

*Be careful to love the truth only.*

2 Thessalonians 2:11-12 says, "And for this reason God will send them strong delusion, that they should believe the lie, that they all may be condemned who did not believe the truth but had pleasure in unrighteousness."

1 John 1:6 says, "If we say that we have fellowship with Him, and walk in darkness, we lie and do not practice the truth."

John 3:19-20 says, "And this is the condemnation, that the light has come into the world, and men loved darkness rather than light, because their deeds were evil. For everyone practicing evil hates the light and does not come to the light, lest his deeds should be exposed."

It may be that you are mixed with light and darkness. There may be areas of darkness in your life about which you are not yet aware of. It is time to wake up!

## How do you get into the light?
*Jesus tells us that we get into the light by "following Him."*

John 8:12 says, "Then Jesus spoke to them again, saying, 'I am the light of the world. He who follows Me shall not walk in darkness, but have the light of life.'"

*How do we "follow Him"?*

Luke 9:23-24 says, "Then He said to *them* all, 'If anyone desires to come after Me, let him deny himself, and take up his cross daily, and follow Me. For whoever desires to save his life will lose it, but whoever loses his life for My sake will save it.'"

*How do we take up our cross?*

Many feel that taking up our cross is simply to suffer. That is not Scriptural. The meaning embedded in Luke 9:23-24 is to "say no to our soul." Our soul is our will, mind and emotions, that

## Chapter 6 – Wounds From Our Own Sin

meaning the soul of our old carnal nature. It is simply to exchange your old carnal nature for Jesus' righteous nature. When we sense our old nature trying to control our lives, then we confess and repent and make a decision to allow God's life and character to prevail through us.

***When Jesus took up His Cross, it was about Him exchanging His righteous nature for your sinful nature.***

Jesus asked the Rich Young Ruler in Matthew 19 to sell all that he had and follow Him. He asked him to take up his cross so that he could follow Him, Jesus, so that the Rich Young Ruler could be in the light. The Ruler refused. Sometimes God has to help us to take up our crosses by allowing suffering.

**A wake up call! God's mercy on those who are in darkness.**
The Lord is giving each one of us a "Wake up call." There are several New Testament Scriptures that talk about waking up, or awakening. Each time the context of those Scripture passages has to do with a call for you and me to wake up from the darkness of sin to living in the light of the Lord. When we are asleep we are in darkness. Being content with some sin in our lives means that we are in darkness, that we are asleep. If we are constantly living in and for the presence and glory of God, we will be in the light, and our sin will just drop off. The warning is strong. Over the years I have personally seen Christian men and women who did not have any desire to be conformed to the image of Christ. I have seen them reap disastrous and weak lives. See what Jesus said about darkness and light in John 3:19-21.

**Romans 13:8-14 (Amplified Bible) says,**

*8 Keep out of debt and owe no man anything, except to love one another; for he who loves his neighbor [who practices loving others] has fulfilled the Law [relating to one's fellowmen, meeting all its requirements].*

*9 The commandments, You shall not commit adultery, You shall not kill, You shall not steal, You shall not covet (have an evil desire), and any other commandment, are*

## Chapter 6 – Wounds From Our Own Sin

*summed up in the single command, You shall love your neighbor as [you do] yourself.*

*10 Love does no wrong to one's neighbor [it never hurts anybody]. Therefore love meets all the requirements and is the fulfilling of the Law.*

*11 Besides this you know what [a critical] hour this is, how it is high time now for you to* **wake up** *out of your sleep (rouse to reality). For salvation (final deliverance) is nearer to us now than when we first believed (adhered to, trusted in, and relied on Christ, the Messiah).*

*12 The night is far gone and the day is almost here. Let us then drop (fling away) the works and deeds of darkness and put on the [full] armor of light.*

*13 Let us live and conduct ourselves honorably and becomingly as in the [open light of] day, not in reveling (carousing) and drunkenness, not in immorality and debauchery (sensuality and licentiousness), not in quarreling and jealousy.*

*14 But clothe yourself with the Lord Jesus Christ (the Messiah), and make no provision for [indulging] the flesh [put a stop to thinking about the evil cravings of your physical nature] to [gratify its] desires (lusts).*

**Ephesians 5:10-17 (Amplified Bible) says,**

*10 And try to learn [in your experience] what is pleasing to the Lord [let your lives be constant proofs of what is most acceptable to Him].*

*11 Take no part in and have no fellowship with the fruitless deeds and enterprises of darkness, but instead [let your lives be so in contrast as to] expose and reprove and convict them.*

*12 For it is a shame even to speak of or mention the things that [such people] practice in secret.*

*13 But when anything is exposed and reproved by the light, it is made visible and clear; and where everything is visible and clear there is light.*

## Chapter 6 – Wounds From Our Own Sin

*14 Therefore He says,* **Awake, O sleeper***, and arise from the dead, and Christ shall shine (make day dawn) upon you and give you light.*
*15 Look carefully then how you walk! Live purposefully and worthily and accurately, not as the unwise and witless, but as wise (sensible, intelligent people),*
*16 Making the very most of the time [buying up each opportunity], because the days are evil.*
*17 Therefore do not be vague and thoughtless and foolish, but understanding and firmly grasping what the will of the Lord is.*

### 1 Corinthians 15:33-34 says,;
*33 Do not be deceived: "Evil company corrupts good habits."*
*34* **Awake to righteousness***, and do not sin; for some do not have the knowledge of God. I speak this to your shame."*

When you awake to who you really are in Christ, the righteousness that He gives you by grace and not by your performance, then that awakening will give you the light and power to go and sin no more. Your focus needs to be on the light and living for God. Do not focus on the sin you are trying not to do, if you do you will be more likely to fall back into that sin. You will have the same experience that the lady caught in adultery had in John chapter 8. She was given the love, power and grace to go and sin no more.

### The definition of sin.
People in general, both believers and non-believers, have misunderstood the true essence of sin. Most people see sin as some horrible moral act. It is that for sure, but I submit that the horrible moral act is more a *result* of sin itself.

## Chapter 6 – Wounds From Our Own Sin

Romans 14:23b, says, "For whatever is not from faith is sin." I submit that sin is doing something that was not originated by God speaking, or not doing something that God has spoken for you to do. Faith always arises from hearing God speak; therefore sin is living without being obedient to what you have heard God speak. Perhaps it may not be hearing God speak currently, but having heard the Word of God, say five years ago that you should forgive, therefore today you forgive as obedience. Maybe you just know it is proper to tithe and give, but you just avoid it because it doesn't seem to make any sense.

**1 Samuel 15:22-23 (KJV) says,**

*22 And Samuel said, Hath the LORD as great delight in burnt offerings and sacrifices, as in obeying the voice of the LORD? Behold, to obey is better than sacrifice, and to hearken than the fat of rams.*

*23 For rebellion is as the sin of witchcraft, and stubbornness is as iniquity and idolatry. Because thou hast rejected the word of the LORD, he hath also rejected thee from being king."*

The sacrifices offered here by Saul were those the ones described in Leviticus as sweet-savor offerings. These had nothing to do with sin, but were rather offerings offered to God for His acceptance and satisfaction. Why then did Samuel compare obedience to this sacrifice? Because, as the story reveals, even in sacrifice there can be an element of self-will, and that can never honor or please God. Only obedience "smells good" to God!

***Sin is defined as missing the mark.***

I submit that the mark is the path that God has for our lives, His will for our lives. More specifically, it has the consequence of not sharing in the prize of the winner. It is as if the person has been aiming at the wrong target. Regardless if they hit their target, they have still missed the mark that God has established and this is the only measurable target that we will be judged by.

Transgressions are defined as "a moral revolt against God," which is seen as the actions that a person takes. These can be

## Chapter 6 – Wounds From Our Own Sin

either intentional or accidental. Either way, they are revolting against God's will.

Iniquities are defined as " morally evil or pervert," which is seen as the evil desires or the flesh that one allows to rule in their hearts. Iniquity is the rejection of God's authority in a person's life, whereby every intent of the heart is bent on evil. Iniquity also carries the meaning of "the consequence or punishment" which results from iniquity.

**All have sinned and fallen short of the glory of God.**
What we have fallen short of is the presence of God, which is what we were created for. The mark we have missed is the presence of God. By sin we have missed that mark as an archer watches his arrow fall short of the target and bulls eye. Our natural state of being is to be in His presence. Our natural way of being cared for is to hear Him speak while we are in His presence. That is the essence of "The just shall sustain their lives by faith" (Hebrews 10:38). Sometimes I refer to that as spiritual agriculture. Sin has separated us from God. Even if you are a Christian you can also continue to be separated from God's presence, His glory, and therefore His provisions for your life will not be forthcoming.

*The first step to the solution is your believing what the Word of God says about sin.*
*1. That sin will keep you from living a normal life.*
*2. That God has given you a way to escape from the  bondage of sin.*

If you believe these two points, then the rest is all in your thinking. Either your thinking is "stinking" or it is disciplined. Your old flesh nature and satanic forces will work on your thinking to cause you to behave in such a way that you deny that your sins have been forgiven. If you are in bondage in some area of your life, take a look at your thinking and see if it lines up with the truth of the Word of God. You will speak as you think, and your life will finally conform to your thinking. Your thinking will create your habits and your speech. Finally, your habits and speech will dictate the course and quality of your life. I am not talking about

Chapter 6 – Wounds From Our Own Sin

some perfect sinless state. I am talking about continually making progress in your walk with the Lord, and when needed, repenting and forgiving your way through life. Also, if you are just going though a period of standing on the promises of God and are going through tribulation for that, do not feel condemned by your problems, just make sure you are attempting to live a life pleasing to the Lord.

**The tragedy of Adam and Eve's sin is the original and perfect example of how one's own sin can bring inner wounds that need God's healing touch.**
These two people had the perfect Father, God Himself, yet their own sin and false perception of God brought about the curse and inner wounds that all of us deal with. Their thinking became tuned to a lie. They bought the lie and even spoke it themselves.

*Satan went to work to cause wounds in the first people, Adam and Eve.*
Adam and Eve were created in the image of God. Satan lied to them in order to create insecurity and inferiority in their souls. Satan was successful with them, and he attempts the same strategy with us. Satan broke their relationship with their Father, God, and in doing so he inflicted wounds in their souls. This is often referred to as "Broken Bridges."

"Now the serpent was more cunning than any beast of the field which the LORD God had made. And he said to the woman, 'Has God indeed said, 'You shall not eat of every tree of the garden'?' And the woman said to the serpent, 'We may eat the fruit of the trees of the garden; but of the fruit of the tree which is in the midst of the garden, God has said, 'You shall not eat it, nor shall you touch it, lest you die.' Then the serpent said to the woman, 'You will not surely die. For God knows that in the day you eat of it your eyes will be opened, and you will be like God, knowing good and evil.' So when the woman saw that the tree was good for food, that it was pleasant to the eyes, and a tree desirable to make one wise, she took of its fruit and ate. She also gave to her husband with her, and he ate. Then the eyes of both of them were opened, and they knew that they were naked; and they sewed fig leaves together and made themselves coverings" (Genesis 3:1-7).

**Satan convinced Eve that God had lied to her.**

Eve even added to God's Words when she said, "You shall not eat it, nor shall you touch it, lest you die." God did not say not to touch it, only not to eat it. I have always seen the Tree of Knowledge of Good and Evil as the mind of reasoning disconnected with self-will from the Word of God. I have always seen the Tree of Life as the Word of God itself.

***Eve felt insecure, feeling that her Father had lied to her.***

She began to think of herself as inferior, and that she had not been made in the image of God. Satan inferred that she was lacking something when he said, "your eyes will be opened, and you will be like God."

Adam and Eve were wounded by the lie. They had lost their Father relationship, and were now living as insecure and inferior people. These wounds have spread to mankind in general. Notice, their wounds did not come from the rejection of their Father, but from their own sin. Also notice that Satan attacked them in their thinking process. That is where the battlefield is, and that is where we need to discipline ourselves.

## The result of sin

***Adam and Eve came under the curse of providing for themselves.***

Like I wrote above, when you are not living in God's glory, you cannot hear Him speak and then His provisions cannot be transferred to you by faith.

Genesis 3:17-19 says, "Then to Adam He said, 'Because you have heeded the voice of your wife, and have eaten from the tree of which I commanded you, saying, 'You shall not eat of it': Cursed is the ground for your sake; In toil you shall eat of it All the days of your life. Both thorns and thistles it shall bring forth for you, And you shall eat the herb of the field. In the sweat of your face you shall eat bread Till you return to the ground, For out of it you were taken; For dust you are, And to dust you shall return.'"

## Chapter 6 – Wounds From Our Own Sin

***Pain of all kinds came upon mankind. Women in many ways have taken the brunt of it. Women have been brutally persecuted and mistreated by men.***

Genesis 3:16 says, "To the woman He said: 'I will greatly multiply your sorrow and your conception; In pain you shall bring forth children; Your desire shall be for your husband, And he shall rule over you."

***Mankind lost the glory of God, the intimate presence of their Father.***

That death, or separation from God the Father, causes a great wound in each one of us.

Genesis 3:23-24 says, "therefore the LORD God sent him out of the garden of Eden to till the ground from which he was taken. So He drove out the man; and He placed cherubim at the east of the garden of Eden, and a flaming sword which turned every way, to guard the way to the tree of life."

Hosea 4:7 says "The more they increased, The more they sinned against Me; I will change their glory into shame."

Romans 3:23 says, "for all have sinned and fall short of the glory of God."

***Mankind died.***

Genesis 2:17 says, "but of the tree of the knowledge of good and evil you shall not eat, for in the day that you eat of it you shall surely die."

The word used for die in Greek means to separate. Adam and Eve were separated spiritually from God because the Holy Spirit "moved out." Adam and Eve eventually died physically because their spirit and soul were separated from their bodies. They died twice.

***Sin caused the birth of the world's first "religion."***

Genesis 3:7 says, "Then the eyes of both of them were opened, and they knew that they were naked; and they sewed fig leaves together and made themselves coverings." These fig leaves were the father of all religion. Religion covers up and attempts to find a way for man to please an angry God. God's solution was the Lamb of God.

Chapter 6 – Wounds From Our Own Sin

Genesis 3:21 says, "Also for Adam and his wife the LORD God made tunics of skin, and clothed them." Blood was shed for Adam and Eve, the blood of a perfect lamb.

***Wounds cause the loss of identity and purpose.***

Isaiah 61:3 says, "To console those who mourn in Zion, To give them beauty for ashes, The oil of joy for mourning, The garment of praise for the spirit of heaviness; That they may be called trees of righteousness, The planting of the LORD, that He may be glorified."

This Scripture, which was part of Jesus' missions statement, could be referring to mourning for actual loses of our life's dreams, loved ones, even our health, etc., but I also believe that we have mourned as captives for the loss of our identity. We are of the race of the New Creation. When we really know who God made us to be is when we will begin to live our lives in a godly way. We will see the miracle of grace which is Christ living His life through us.

**It's more than just about you!**

Being self-centered and selfish always causes a person to think only about their own welfare, their own feelings and well being. I have learned, and am still learning, to think outside my own little box of "me." Everything you do and say has an eternal affect on other people. In our previous chapter we covered generational curses. That chapter primarily dealt with the curses that have been passed down to you through sin. What about the curses you are passing down, right now? You are part of a chain of legacy. Actually, it is more than that. You are part of a chain in eternity. God trusts you to sow blessings for those coming behind you, both in your children, families, and for the Body of Christ in general.

***We subconsciously create legacies with everything we do and say.***

Create a legacy for those in your realm of influence, a legacy of love and trust in God in all circumstances, especially those that are difficult. Be a person who awakes each day with the passion to give God and those around you a "good day." Don't always look for God and others to give you a "good day." This sowing and

## Chapter 6 – Wounds From Our Own Sin

reaping principle will not only bless you, but millions of others. Be a hilarious giver, not only of money, but also of love, joy, and encouragement. 2 Corinthians 9:7 (Amplified Bible) says, "Let each one [give] as he has made up his own mind and purposed in his heart, not reluctantly or sorrowfully or under compulsion, for God loves (He takes pleasure in, prizes above other things, and is unwilling to abandon or to do without) a cheerful (joyous, "prompt to do it") giver [whose heart is in his giving]."

**The wounds of your sin.**
*Wounds come from sowing and reaping.*
    We will go into the sowing of judgments, vows and soul ties in later chapters. These are three very powerful issues that cause inner wounds in one's life. It is important to know that whatever we sow, we will also reap. What we reap because of our sin causes an inner wound. That includes everything in life, too many subjects to cover. Just take an inventory of your life on a daily basis of what you are sowing, on how you are treating others, and what you are speaking. As we sow bad things through our lives, we will also reap that same bad things, and they will cause wounds that need to be healed in your own being and in those attached to your legacy. The safest way to live your life is to make sure that everything you do and say is based upon love as defined by Jesus.
    *God set up this universe to produce by sowing and reaping.*
    Genesis 8:22 says, "While the earth remains, Seedtime and harvest, Cold and heat, Winter and summer, And day and night Shall not cease."
    Galatians 6:7 says, "Do not be deceived, God is not mocked; for whatever a man sows, that he will also reap."
    Luke 6:38 says, "Give, and it will be given to you: good measure, pressed down, shaken together, and running over will be put into your bosom. For with the same measure that you use, it will be measured back to you."
    2 Corinthians 9:6 says, "But this I say: He who sows sparingly will also reap sparingly, and he who sows bountifully will also reap bountifully."

## Chapter 6 – Wounds From Our Own Sin

**Rebellion from authority of any kind causes wounds.**
Proverbs 17:11 says, "An evil man seeks only rebellion; Therefore a cruel messenger will be sent against him."

Hebrews 3:15 says, "while it is said: 'Today, if you will hear His voice, Do not harden your hearts as in the rebellion [the Wilderness journey of the Israelites].'"

*Jesus made a big point of teaching about respecting authority, which is the opposite of rebellion.*

*Two stories about those who opposed Moses' authority.*

One of the Old Testament examples is in Numbers 12, when Miriam and Aaron spoke against Moses. "Why then were you not afraid to speak against my servant Moses? The anger of the LORD burned against them, and he left them. When the cloud lifted from above the Tent, there stood Miriam--leprous, like snow. Aaron turned towards her and saw that she had leprosy" (Numbers 12:8b-10, NIV). The penalty was serious!

Again, in Numbers 16, it tells about the rebellion of Korah with Dathan and Abiram and the 250 leaders (well known men of distinction) against Moses. The earth opened up and swallowed them alive, them and their households.

When we oppose God's authority either directly or indirectly through His delegated authorities, we are bringing the curse of rebellion into our lives and the lives of those attached to our legacy.

My parents were humble, obedient, hard working, good moral people who believed in God. They were immigrants who appreciated living in America every day of their lives. They had not one bit of rebellion in their hearts. Nevertheless, I went into rebellion as a teenager and was not redeemed for more than 20 years until I met the Lord when I was 39 years old. Why? It was a legacy I had inherited from one of my grandparents. However, one of my other grandparents was not only a godly man, but he was also a passionate church planter. In those last moments as he was preparing to go to Heaven, he said that he saw the angel Gabriel come to take him.

## Chapter 6 – Wounds From Our Own Sin

**Covering a wound with self-righteousness.**
Self-righteousness usually results from one attempting to cover a wound. When confronted directly by God, Job eventually fell on his face, crying, "I heard about You before, but now I have seen you face to face, and I repent!" Job had become self-righteous, like many of us who get a small taste of God. Job's friends were even worse than Job. They thought they had figured out that their performance before God would keep them well and prosperous. That was their orthodoxy and doctrine. They told Job that he would not be suffering unless there was hidden sin in his life. God was not pleased with them at all. They had sown a judgment. However, it seems as though Job interceded for them to protect their outcome. Job's friends had a partial truth in that how they lived their lives could indeed foreshadow their outcome, however, as they learned, that kind of "concrete thinking" misses God's primary purposes for life. We have a good resource on Job: Job's Journey available at our web site http://www.isob-bible.org/job/job-book-2.htm.

**The solution.**
I believe that Scripture gives us the solution for sin from many different points of view. The discussion below in Romans chapters 7 and 8 comes from one very important point of view. One of my other favorites is embedded in 1 John 1:7, which says, "But if we walk in the light as He is in the light, we have fellowship with one another, and the blood of Jesus Christ His Son cleanses us from all sin." As I wrote in the beginning of this chapter, it is vital to "stay in the light," by continually taking up our cross. If we do that we become addicted to the light and sin just falls off. We become disinterested in sinful ways and we crave more and more of the light. As 1 John 1:7 says, "we have fellowship one with another..." That means not only fellowship with God through the Holy Spirit, but with other believers who also radiate the light. I cannot explain the experience, but when we experience light, we change.

## Chapter 6 – Wounds From Our Own Sin

In Romans chapter 7, the apostle Paul felt the horrible final judgment of his own sin, that being "condemnation." Condemnation is like the judge of the highest supreme court making his final decree of guilty, and there is no higher court to which you may appeal. Then he asked the question in Romans 7:24, "O wretched man that I am! Who will deliver me from this body of death?" The "body of death" was a horrible method of execution for those who have been convicted of murder. The authorities would strap the dead corpse to the convicted killer until the body of death would spread disease, rot the killer's body and he would die, a slow and painful death.

The answer was, Romans 7:25 which says, "I thank God—[I can be delivered] through Jesus Christ our Lord! So then, with the mind I myself serve the law of God, but with the flesh the law of sin."

Romans 8:1-4 goes on to say, "There is therefore now no condemnation to those who are in Christ Jesus, who do not walk according to the flesh, but according to the Spirit. For the law of the Spirit of life in Christ Jesus has made me free from the law of sin and death. For what the law could not do in that it was weak through the flesh, God did by sending His own Son in the likeness of sinful flesh, on account of sin: He condemned sin in the flesh, that the righteous requirement of the law might be fulfilled in us who do not walk according to the flesh but according to the Spirit."

***Walking in the Spirit is the discipline marked out here by Paul.***

That means to determine to live a life pleasing to the Lord, to obey Him and honor Him. It also means that when we miss it and sin, that He is quick to forgive. However, that forgiveness is meant to keep us on the path of walking out a righteous life, not a sloppy life.

***You are forgiven!***

The word "forgive" as defined by the Strong's Concordance means: Aphiemi, or separation. One of its root meanings is to die, to murder. To die means to separate. To be forgiven means that your sins have been "removed by surgery," they have been separated from you and put on Jesus. He bore your sins. He suffered the consequence of your sin on your behalf.

1 John 1:9 says, "If we confess our sins, He is faithful and just to forgive us our sins and to cleanse us from all unrighteousness."

Isaiah 53:10 says, "Yet it pleased the LORD to bruise Him; He has put Him to grief. When You make His soul an offering for sin, He shall see His seed, He shall prolong His days, And the pleasure of the LORD shall prosper in His hand."

*You must forgive yourself.*

If you do not agree with God's forgiveness for you, you will not forgive yourself for your past sin, and Satan will keep you in guilt and condemnation. Often it is not easy to forgive yourself. The solution is to simply believe the Word of God instead of your own feelings and emotions.

*We all need to realize the deep, deep truth about our co-crucifixion with Christ.*

Galatians 2:20 says, "I have been crucified with Christ; it is no longer I who live, but Christ lives in me; and the life which I now live in the flesh I live by faith in the Son of God, who loved me and gave Himself for me."

If you really believe that then you will live like that. How can a dead man sin? If Christ is alive in you, He cannot sin. You are no longer "a sinner," even though you sin from time to time. You are a born again child of God and a member of a new race, the New Creation in Christ Jesus. Your old "self" was crucified, it has realized the penalty of death already. Your old man has a death certificate in the heavenlies. You also have a birth certificate in the heavenlies, Psalm 87:5. You are not a dual personality. The "flesh" that wants to sin is simply the old thinking in your mind. It is like a recording that needs to be erased and recorded over.

*How do you stop the cycle of sin?*

It is all about "stinking thinking." The truth will make you free, but you have to get your mind renewed to the truth. You have been crucified with Christ, the Holy Spirit does live in you and He brings His holiness with Him. Go on a fast from "stinking thinking" and your life will conform to the image of Jesus. Romans 12:1-2 makes it clear that we need a discipline to renew our minds, and primarily the Word of God replacing our old thinking does that. Memorize the Word, confess it and meditate upon it.

Be honest with God about your sin. Stay in the Word so that it may be a mirror to convict you of sin. Then confess it to God and enjoy the wonderful healing that will result!

I personally know a man who was completely delivered, quickly, from one of the most addictive sins known, pornography. When he realized, as a new Christian, that this was unpleasing to God, he quickly repented and decided to bring this into the light. The "feeling" of freedom felt so good to him that he became addicted to the Word of God. This became his exchanged passion, and he is growing in the Lord.

Be sensitive to repent, not only of your moral sins, but also of your unwillingness to make Jesus the king and ruler of your entire life. Repent for the selfishness and self-centerness of your flesh. Repent for exalting your emotions and feelings over the Word of God. Allow God to change you into the image of Jesus, the image of love.

Most of all, wake up!

# Chapter 7
## Judgments And Vows
Ways to stay in bondage.

In John 8:3-16 there is a story of the woman caught in adultery and brought before Jesus for judgment. When you read the story, you will see that the Pharisees wanted judgment, but Jesus gave her light.

"When Jesus had raised Himself up and saw no one but the woman, He said to her, 'Woman, where are those accusers of yours? Has no one condemned you?' She said, 'No one, Lord.' And Jesus said to her, 'Neither do I condemn [final condemnation] you; go and sin no more. Then Jesus spoke to them again, saying, 'I am the light of the world. He who follows Me shall not walk in darkness, but have the light of life'" (John 8:10-12).

Jesus did not come to give a new law; He came to bring a whole new way of living which is called "walking in the light" or "walking in the Spirit." The best the Law can do is to convict us of sin, but it cannot remove it. The light cleanses us from all sin. The light reveals the blood of Jesus that washed our sins away. 1 John 1:7 says, "But if we walk in the light as He is in the light, we have fellowship with one another, and the blood of Jesus Christ His Son cleanses us from all sin."

In a later chapter of this book we will cover the idea of walking in the light and walking in the Spirit. One of the keys is to "follow Jesus." This woman called Jesus "Lord," which was her commitment to follow Him.

If Jesus' mission is to encourage people to walk in the light, which is the opposite of judgment, then that should also be our mission.

**What is judgment? There is a dangerous judgment and a righteous judgment.**
The New Testament word used for judgment means final condemnation or damnation as a judge would issue a final decree

## Chapter 7 – Judgments And Vows

in the courtroom. Only God can issue final judgments. Only God knows how some person will end up. Some of the wicked criminals have been gloriously saved and have received God's mercy. Mercy triumphs over judgment. We need to be careful not to judge people in this sense. We should not be holding final decrees over them. Judgment starts with our mind, but is confirmed by our words. Even if you have a "feeling" about another person, do not speak it out, but rather give it to God and ask Him to protect you from judging that person. Be honest with God about your feelings and He will help you work through it. Be very sensitive lest you will pay a high price.

Romans 14:10 says, "But why do you judge your brother? Or why do you show contempt for your brother? For we shall all stand before the judgment seat of Christ."

James 4:11-15 says, "Do not speak evil of one another, brethren. He who speaks evil of a brother and judges his brother, speaks evil of the law and judges the law. But if you judge the law, you are not a doer of the law but a judge. There is one Lawgiver, who is able to save and to destroy. Who are you to judge another?

Matthew 7:1-4 says, "Judge not, that you be not judged. For with what judgment you judge, you will be judged; and with the measure you use, it will be measured back to you. And why do you look at the speck in your brother's eye, but do not consider the plank in your own eye? Or how can you say to your brother, 'Let me remove the speck from your eye'; and look, a plank is in your own eye?"

The speck that you are criticizing and judging in your brother's eye is perhaps his fault or sin. However, Jesus said here that focusing on that sin is the plank in your eye. Which is more serious, the speck of your brother's sin or the plank of your judgment and criticism? Like my friend and co-editor Michael Vincent says, "Judgment is like throwing a ping pong ball at a wall and having it come back and hit you like a bowling ball."

***We should not even "judge" ourselves.***

*1 Corinthians 4:3 says,*

## Chapter 7 – Judgments And Vows

> *"3 But with me it is a very small thing that I should be judged by you or by a human court. In fact, I do not even judge myself (said Paul)."*

We all need to be convicted of sin by the gently and loving Holy Spirit so that we may have that sin removed by confession and repentance. However if we judge ourselves we are taking God's place and we will suffer.

**Some have told me that ungodly judgments are their most common sin!**

Judgments used in the wrong way can be very dangerous as this chapter goes on to describe. There is a sowing and reaping principle involved and we can be in danger if we take judgment into our own hands. However, in an effort to really hit the mark, I want to attempt to define judgment from a Biblical viewpoint. While we need to be very cautious about wrong judgment, we also need the true Biblical viewpoint in order to be protected from people with evil intentions.

### *Righteous judgment.*

Jesus said, "Do not judge according to appearance, but judge with righteous judgment" (John 7:24). Jesus said to judge, but to do it righteously. The only thing righteous judgment could mean to me is to judge just exactly like Jesus does.

All judgment has been entrusted to Jesus, and Jesus is the Word of God. "For the Father judges no one, but has committed all judgment to the Son" (John 5:22). Jesus was rarely critical. Some of the exceptions were when He confronted the Pharisees.

### *How does Jesus judge?*

He judges according to the Word. He took the penalty and the judgment for everyone's sin. That is His judgment for people. It will continue to be His judgment for them until their death, and then they will be judged for whether or not they accepted Him as their sacrifice.

However, Jesus does judge and condemn demons, devils, and Satan himself as in the Book of Revelation and also when He confronted them in the Gospels. He always separated the person from the devil or demon.

### *Judgment on the flesh and the demonic world.*

Bad fruit may or may not be demonic activity. We know that demons cannot "possess" a child of God, but they sure can influence, to varying degrees, their behavior.

What you have seen or experienced in another person may not be demonic but may be their old flesh nature. What is the judgment on that? It is the same as Jesus' judgment. Confess the Word for these people, as an example, "I have been crucified with Christ; it is no longer I who live, but Christ lives in me; and the life which I now live in the flesh I live by faith in the Son of God, who loved me and gave Himself for me" (Galatians 2:20). Call those things that are not as though they were, Romans 4:17. Speak the Word of God over the victim for victory and against the demons and/or the flesh for their destruction.

Righteous judgment is having mercy for the sinner, confessing their sin on Jesus, and at the same time, speaking the Word of judgment against the active demon and the flesh. That kind of judgment will tend to separate the human from the demonic activity and/or the flesh nature. 1 John 5:16 says, "If anyone sees his brother sinning a sin which does not lead to death, he will ask, and He will give him life for those who commit sin not leading to death. There is sin leading to death. I do not say that he should pray about that."

If we sense a negative criticism flaring up against another, and even if we have discernment regarding an inappropriate activity in another, our judgment, our righteous judgment is to confess the truth over them. It is to confess that Jesus is the Lamb that bore their sin. Righteous judgment is similar to forgiveness. It is putting another person's sin on Jesus, and believing that Jesus will redeem that person, perhaps even aided by your testimony and righteous judgment.

## Chapter 7 – Judgments And Vows

### *The benefits of judging righteously.*

Isaiah 58:6, 9-11 says, "*Is* this not the fast that I have chosen: To loose the bonds of wickedness, to undo the heavy burdens, to let the oppressed go free, and that you break every yoke?"

"Then you shall call, and the LORD will answer; You shall cry, and He will say, 'Here I *am*.' "If you take away the yoke from your midst, The pointing of the finger, and speaking wickedness, *If* you extend your soul to the hungry And satisfy the afflicted soul, Then your light shall dawn in the darkness, And your darkness shall *be* as the noonday. The LORD will guide you continually, And satisfy your soul in drought, And strengthen your bones; You shall be like a watered garden, And like a spring of water, whose waters do not fail."

### **Judgment is not**:

1. Discerning of spirits as described in 1 Corinthians 12:10 which is a gift given by the Holy Spirit for ministry purposes. God may give you, as He has given me, and millions of others in the past, a supernatural revelation, either in the Word or just in your spirit, that there is a certain type of spirit or demon operating in a person or in a situation. This is not judgment; this is simply listening to God for wisdom. It may also be the revelation by the Word of Knowledge to know something about that person's life. Usually its purpose is for healing the situation and/or helping you to construct boundaries in your life.

Some judgments may start with discernment. For example, God gives someone discernment to speak the truth into someone else's life, but instead of being obedient they combine the discernment with fear and their own stinking thinking, and it then turns into a judgment. For what God meant for good they turn into evil.

Discernment produces conviction, which is good, but judgment produces condemnation. Judgments are often based out of fear. There is a difference between godly judgment and being judgmental in an ungodly manner. I know people who have a supernatural gift of discernment, yet they are not judgmental.

## Chapter 7 – Judgments And Vows

Be very careful when judging another person. Very often we can misjudge others because we tend to use ourselves as the standard for judging others.

Romans 2:1 says, "Therefore you are inexcusable, O man, whoever you are who judge, for in whatever you judge another you condemn yourself; for you who judge practice the same things."

2. Detection of bad fruit in others. Detection is simply recognizing a trait in another person by experience. For instance, if you have seen a pattern of con artists who raise money for ministry in a certain manner, you certainly do not want to get involved. However, that is not judgment, it is simply being smart, detecting their fruit, and staying away.

*As an example, Jezebel spirits usually operate in people who exercise inordinate authority and manipulation.*

I have seen this quite often. When I see it, I detect it, and just take note of it. This is not judgment because I am simply listening to God and waiting to act or not act in obedience to what He says. If God had not revealed this spirit to me one time in my life, I know that my life would have been devastated. He saved me by discernment and detection. Detection and discernment of this kind surely lets me know how to pray and how to construct boundaries for my family and myself. My "judgment" on this is: I confess that Jesus is the Lamb that bore the sin of that person, but I pray the Scripture against the demon unto its condemnation.

*Jesus warned us to look at fruit for our safe keeping.*

Matthew 7:15-23 says, "Beware of false prophets, who come to you in sheep's clothing, but inwardly they are ravenous wolves. You will know them by their fruits. Do men gather grapes from thornbushes or figs from thistles? Even so, every good tree bears good fruit, but a bad tree bears bad fruit. A good tree cannot bear bad fruit, nor can a bad tree bear good fruit. Every tree that does not bear good fruit is cut down and thrown into the fire. Therefore by their fruits you will know them. Not everyone who says to Me, 'Lord, Lord,' shall enter the kingdom of heaven, but he who does the will of My Father in heaven. Many will say to Me in that day, 'Lord, Lord, have we not prophesied in Your name, cast out demons in Your name, and done many wonders in Your name?' And then I will declare to them, 'I never knew you; depart from Me, you who practice lawlessness!'"

Romans 16:17-20 says, "Now I urge you, brethren, note those who cause divisions and offenses, contrary to the doctrine which you learned, and avoid them. For those who are such do not serve our Lord Jesus Christ, but their own belly, and by smooth words and flattering speech deceive the hearts of the simple. For your obedience has become known to all. Therefore I am glad on your behalf; but I want you to be wise in what is good, and simple concerning evil. And the God of peace will crush Satan under your feet shortly. The grace of our Lord Jesus Christ *be* with you. Amen."

However, even with discerning of spirits and detection you should not run around broadcasting what you have discovered. You should hold your information primarily for intercession and for the protection of those around you. Once you begin to focus on the wrong you see in people and discuss it with others, you could be in danger of being a judge in the dangerous sense of the term. You would also be guilty of gossip and slander. God reserves judgment for Himself, and you are robbing God of His position, which is very dangerous. There is only one lawgiver and judge, the One who is able to save and destroy. Christ is called to judge because He is qualified: He alone has all the information. He alone is just.

Make sure that you put your feelings on the altar and ask God to show you some bitter root that you may have towards others or yourself that could be causing unhealthy judgment that could be disguised as fruit inspection. I act upon what I believe about myself and judge others out of that belief. If I believe that I am rejected then I will get myself rejected. I will teach people how to treat me based on the judgments I have made. It is a self-fulfilling prophecy that operates by the power of the law that we will reap what we sow.

## Some examples of dangerous and inordinate judgment.
### *Some good examples are Job's friends.*

Three of the four friends thought that they knew the reason for Job's sufferings. They told him that the reason he was suffering was because he had sin in his life. Only one, Elihu, spoke truth to Job and that was because he was anointed by the Holy Spirit. God spoke to Job's friends in Job 42:7 which says, "After the LORD had said these things to Job, he said to Eliphaz the Temanite, 'I am angry with you and your two friends, because you have not spoken of me what is right, as my servant Job has.'" Notice all three friends attempted to help Job understand his horrible circumstances, but God was angry with them because they misrepresented God and judged Job. Job 32:3 says, "Also against his three friends his wrath was aroused, because they had found no answer, and *yet* had condemned Job."

We never really know the complex issues in another's life. We may know 98%, but only God knows everything in someone's heart. I know many who have been grossly misjudged and misunderstood by others. It would have been better for these "judges" just to take their suspicions to God and leave the judgment to Him. Our judgment, if it does not come as a revelation from God, is usually clouded with our own complex personalities; we usually judge out of our own motives, Romans 2:1. Judgment can be in one's heart, but when the words are spoken it is much more serious.

Another example of dangerous judgment is the way Moses handled the provision of water from the rock in Numbers 20:10. "And Moses and Aaron gathered the assembly together before the rock; and he said to them, 'Hear now, you rebels! Must we bring water for you out of this rock?'" God wanted to give the people water out of His mercy and told Moses not to strike the rock. Moses conveyed the idea that God was mad. Because of this Moses did not enter the Promise Land. Heavy!!

## Chapter 7 – Judgments And Vows

**The danger of unrighteous judgment.**
We are called to be witnesses. A witness will bring testimony to a court. A witness is not the judge. Our testimony about our brother is that Jesus took the judgment of their sin. Even more, we should shudder at even attempting to know for sure that sin is active in their lives. Rather we should judge ourselves that we do not come under judgment.

For example, if you see a brother who has a wayward child, it would be easy to "judge" and say, "Oh, maybe brother so and so was not a good parent and that is why his child is a prodigal." That could very easily come back to curse your own child. You should rather say, "That child is the seed of the righteous and the seed of the righteous is blessed, taught of the Lord, and is delivered." "Do not be deceived, God is not mocked; for whatever a man sows, that he will also reap" (Galatians 6:7).

We need to error on the side of mercy and be harmless as doves, and at the same time, be wise as serpents so that Satan cannot take undue advantage over us. When you judge righteously, the law of sowing and reaping will bring righteous judgment back to you as a reward.

*A friend of mine told me a story of a horrible reaping of judgments he had witnessed.*

There was a boy who used to laugh and mock at people who were overweight. He really gave them a hard time. He developed a thyroid problem and gained so much weight that he became obese without even trying.

I have personally witnessed people in churches judge and condemn people who were divorced. They had no idea whether the divorce was Scriptural or not, or anything about the circumstances. They had taken a Pharisee-type view. We have witnessed many of these people experience divorce in their lives and/or in their children's lives. You will usually reap the same type of judgment that you sow.

## Chapter 7 – Judgments And Vows

**Vows.**

The subject of vows is a challenge for me to write about. Vows are statements we make about we will do, or be like, or will never do, or never be like. Vows are made from our old "flesh" or Adamic nature. Sometimes they can be made with a decent motive, but in making them from our old nature, we may be bringing a bad judgment into lives. To be sure, and like all of our words, they extend into the spiritual world and can be very dangerous.

Having said that, we should always be aware of God's sovereignty. We cannot possible put God in a box on this issue.

A judgment tears others down and a vow builds me up. The judgment says look at them, the vow says what about me? We make vows to help us feel better about ourselves. The vow is permanent in nature; therefore it is not in our control once we have made the vow. For instance, if you judged your father for being critical, you might vow that you will never be that way. But because we reap what we sow we end up being critical. Sometimes it takes years to manifest itself into our lives but then it becomes very strong until we break the judgment and renounce the vow in Jesus' name. So many of our bad attitudes are rooted in our vows we made when we were judging others.

When we stop judging it doesn't mean what others have done is right; it just sets us free from the cords that bind us to them because of our judgments and inner vows.

The most devastating judgments and vows we make are against our parents. Deuteronomy 5:16 says, "Honor your father and your mother, as the LORD your God has commanded you, that your days may be long, and that it may be well with you in the land which the LORD your God is giving you." To honor means to obey (within godly limits of course), to do your best to try to respect, it means to love, cherish, and to forgive. Sometimes parents have hurt us but God tells us to love from from His heart. If we judge our parent with an evil heart we are dishonoring them. God's law of vows will take effect and life will not go well with us.

We either become exactly the opposite of everything we judge: by upholding every standard we have established and fulfilling every vow we have ever made and as a result we become completely self-righteous and bound to performance. Or we become exactly like everything we judged: by violating every standard we have established and breaking every vow we have made and as a result we become self-condemning and bound to shame.

Matthew 5:33-37 says, "Again you have heard that it was said to those of old, 'You shall not swear falsely, but shall perform your oaths to the Lord.' But I say to you, do not swear at all: neither by heaven, for it is God's throne; nor by the earth, for it is His footstool; nor by Jerusalem, for it is the city of the great King. Nor shall you swear by your head, because you cannot make one hair white or black. But let your 'Yes' be 'Yes,' and your 'No,' 'No.' For whatever is more than these is from the evil one."

When a person makes a vow, they have then relied on their own strength to fulfill it. This brings a curse. Jeremiah 17:5 says "Thus says the LORD: 'Cursed *is* the man who trusts in man And makes flesh his strength, Whose heart departs from the LORD.'"

While Colossians chapter 2:20-23 primarily deals with the religious works of the flesh, it also gives us an example of the vanity of trusting in our flesh, which includes vows.

**Colossians 2:20-23 (Amplified Bible) says,**

*20 If then you have died with Christ to material ways of looking at things and have escaped from the world's crude and elemental notions and teachings of externalism, why do you live as if you still belong to the world? [Why do you submit to rules and regulations?--such as]*

*21 Do not handle [this], Do not taste [that], Do not even touch [them],*

*22 Referring to things all of which perish with being used. To do this is to follow human precepts and doctrines.*

*23 Such [practices] have indeed the outward appearance [that popularly passes] for wisdom, in promoting self-imposed rigor of devotion and delight in self-humiliation and severity of discipline of the body, but*

## Chapter 7 – Judgments And Vows

*they are of no value in checking the indulgence of the flesh (the lower nature). [Instead, they do not honor God but serve only to indulge the flesh.]*

**How do you make a commitment without it becoming a vow?**
Marriage vow and other vows that are ordained by God are good and healthy, but even then we should make them counting on God's grace and power and not our own abilities. So it is with other commitments. We should come to God and ask Him to conform our lives to His image, and to bring about His purposes in our lives. Then we should discipline our lives to become and stay intimate with Him, or to "abide in Him" as stated in John chapter 15.

**The following is a quote from <u>Inner Healing</u> by Dunklin.**
*Whatever judgments we sow against another, we will receive from others. Knowing this, we should desire to sow love and mercy wherever we go, knowing we will receive love and mercy in return.*

*Whatever is incubated within our souls is created in our circumstances. Whatever we project out through our souls to others is received by their souls and sent back to us. For this reason, we should keep our souls soaked in Divine love.*

*"Who shall bring a charge against God's elect? It is God who justifies" (Romans 8:33).*

**The following is a quote from the devotion, <u>The Cross of Christ</u>, June 22.**
*The Unchanging Law Of Judgment*
*"With what judgment you judge, you will be judged; and with the measure you use, it will be measured back to you" (Matthew 7:2).*

*This statement is not some haphazard theory, but it is an eternal law of God. Whatever judgment you give will be the very way you are judged. There is a difference*

## Chapter 7 – Judgments And Vows

*between retaliation and retribution. Jesus said that the basis of life is retribution- "with the measure you use, it will be measured back to you." If you have been shrewd in finding out the short-comings of others, remember that will be exactly how you will be measured. The way you pay is the way life will pay you back. This eternal law works from God's throne down to us (see Psalm 18:25-26). Romans 2:1 applies it in even a more definite way by saying that the one who criticizes another is guilty of the very same thing. God looks not only at the act itself, but also at the possibility of committing it, which He sees by looking at our hearts.*

It is wise to begin this process of breaking judgments and vows with the root judgments we have made against our parents. These have affected our lives more than any other judgments we have made. Pray and allow the Holy Spirit to show us what judgments and vows we have made against our parents. Then repeat these prayers to break the power they have in our lives.

**Breaking judgments prayer:**

I judged _____ for _____.
**I break that judgment in Jesus name.**

*I vowed that_____. I renounce that vow in Jesus name.*

117

# Chapter 8
# Soul Ties
Another way to stay in bondage

Soul ties [16] are formed when two or more persons become bonded together. Soul ties can be good or evil, either holy or profane. God has sanctioned soul ties through the bonding of children with parents, husbands with wives, friends with friends, and Christians with Christians. Soul ties approved by God represent the bonding of persons together with bonds of agape love. Soul ties were meant to bring the bridge of agape love. What God intended for good, evil counterfeits. Evil soul ties are the bridge that brings evil into your life.

There are different levels of soul ties. The more powerful soul ties like sexual, marriage, and family soul ties actually make each party vulnerable to the curses and blessings of the other parties. For instance, if a 16-year old boy has sex with a prostitute, then that boy has become vulnerable to all of the curses of not only that prostitute, but also of all the other men with whom that prostitute had sex. The prostitute, and therefore the boy, is soul-tied to thousands or millions of other people and is vulnerable to their curses as well. There are also soul ties that are less powerful, such as friendship ties, which we will discuss in this chapter.

Good soul ties are meant to be established, first through the relationship between parents and children. As the healthy child matures, he can then establish healthy soul ties with a limited number of close friends. Later, he becomes ready to establish his closest soul tie, through marriage. After this, the married couple can establish mutual soul ties with other Christians.

---

[16] Much of the information in this chapter is taking from the book <u>Inner Healing, Session Eight Judgments and Soul Ties</u>, which is used by permission. Copyright \* 1992 by Dunklin Memorial Church – Used by permission ISOB.

## Chapter 8 - Soul Ties

**Marriage soul ties.**
Ephesians 5:31 (ASV) says, "For this cause shall a man leave his father and mother, and shall cleave to his wife; and the two shall become one flesh." A husband and wife are bonded together by love.

Matthew 19:6 says, "So then, they are no longer two but one flesh. Therefore what God has joined together, let not man separate."

The ideal marriage is one in which God has joined a husband and wife. If God has joined a husband and wife, which is not always the case, and divorce has separated them, then much pain, trauma, and sorrow is experienced resulting in inner wounds. Even in the case of divorce where God has not joined the couple, soul ties are formed which must be broken. In either case, wounds of rejection and low self-esteem are likely.

**Parent/child soul ties.**
When the soul tie isn't established between the parents and the child, the child is likely to spend the rest of his or her life trying to reconnect the missing tie. Through continual searching, the child becomes vulnerable to substitute soul ties, most of which are evil.

Joseph's family came to Egypt looking for food there due to a famine in their land. This was while Joseph was a leader in Egypt. He greeted his brothers while hiding his identity. His plan was to trick the brothers by putting a valuable silver cup in Benjamin's pack and have him caught as a thief, thus bringing Benjamin back to Egypt and inducing his father Jacob to come as well. When this happened, Judah begged Joseph, who was still disguised, to allow Benjamin to return. Judah made his case stating that his father Jacob had a soul tie with Benjamin, and breaking that would cause Jacob to die.

Genesis 44:30-31 says, "Now therefore, when I come to your servant my father, and the lad is not with us, since his life is bound up in the lad's life [his soul knit with the lad's soul], it will happen, when he sees that the lad is not with us, that he will die. So your

## Chapter 8 - Soul Ties

servants will bring down the gray hair of your servant our father with sorrow to the grave."

When a child is born, the infant should be bonded to its parents. A healthy soul tie should be formed which ministers love and security to that child throughout life. This soul tie serves to stabilize the child's personality. However, there are cases where one of the parents does not release the soul tie as the adult child enters into marriage and requires release. I have seen older men totally controlled by a toxic mother, resulting in a marriage that never matures into a godly union.

## Friendship soul ties.

Friendship soul ties can be a blessing if between two godly people. Even then they are the weakest of the types of soul ties. They are not always spiritual in nature and do not always act as a conduit of curses.

### *Jonathan and David.*

1 Samuel 18:1 says, "Now when he had finished speaking to Saul, the soul of Jonathan was knit to the soul of David, and Jonathan loved him as his own soul."

This is another type of soul tie that is pure and is based upon love. Proverbs 18:24 says, "A man who has friends must himself be friendly, but there is a friend who sticks closer than a brother." This is a special kind of loyalty that exists between devoted friends.

## Christian soul ties.

Ephesians 4:16 says, "...from whom the whole body, joined and knit together by what every joint supplies, according to the effective working by which every part does its share, causes growth of the body for the edifying of itself in love."

The relationship between Christians is compared to the relationship between the various parts of the human body. These soul ties enable the body of Christ to mature and fulfill its calling.

Christian and friendship soul ties do not have the level of potential for negative affects that some of the others have.

## Chapter 8 - Soul Ties

However, Scripture does warn us to not have close relationships with people who have ungodly lifestyles, as they can affect us in a very negative way.

**Evil companion soul ties.**
1 Corinthians 15:33 (NASB) says, "Do not be deceived; bad company corrupts good morals." Proverbs 22:24-25 (NASB) says, "Do not associate with a man given to anger; or go with a hot-tempered man, or you will learn his ways and find a snare for yourself (for your soul)."

Soul ties with evil companions will so ensnare a person that he/she will become entangled in the grasp of wickedness. Our friends influence us; therefore it is important to choose the right ones.

**Demonic soul ties.**
1 Corinthians 6:16 (NASB) says, "Or do you not know that the one who joins himself to a prostitute is one body with her? For He says, the two shall become one flesh."

Demonic soul ties formed imitate the soul ties of the good and holy ties that are founded upon love. Good soul ties are founded upon love. Demonic soul ties are founded upon lust.

For example, sexual relationships outside of marriage forge demonic soul ties. Through adultery or fornication, an evil soul tie is created in lust. This demonic soul tie destroys the holy union that was based upon mutual love and trust.

Romans 1:26-27 (NASB) says, "For this reason God gave them over to degrading passions; for their women exchanged their natural function for that which is unnatural, and in the same way also the men abandoned the natural function of the woman and burned in their desire for one another, men with men committing indecent acts and receiving in their own persons the due penalty of their error."

Perverse soul ties are also formed between persons of the same sex. Homosexuals and lesbians are motivated by lust, though they may call themselves lovers.

Also, perverse soul ties extend themselves to those formed between human beings and animals. The ultimate expression of perversion is bestiality, lying carnally with animals. Some soul ties with animals fall short of bestiality. They are characterized by an inordinate affection for animals.

**Perverted family soul ties.**

Jesus spoke often about the danger of bonding with your family. In a perfect world, family soul ties are beneficial and a blessing. However, if you are trying to walk out your life with Jesus and your family is not, they can have a major negative influence on your spiritual life, even causing you to backslide and reject God completely.

Luke 14:26 (Amplified Bible) says, "If anyone comes to Me and does not hate his [own] father and mother [in the sense of indifference to or relative disregard for them in comparison with his attitude toward God] and [likewise] his wife and children and brothers and sisters--[yes] and even his own life also--he cannot be My disciple." The soul tie between a parent and a child is healthy and beneficial, except when it continues into the adult life of the child. When a son or daughter is ready for marriage, the soul tie with the parents must be terminated in order for a soul tie of marriage to be formed.

When the father gives his daughter in marriage, he severs the soul tie with her in preference to her husband. When the soul tie is not severed between the parent and the child at the proper time, that which was good and beneficial becomes evil through control and possessiveness.

Sexual perverseness within family relations occurs when there is incest between father/daughter, mother/son, brother/sister, father-in-law/daughter-in-law, mother-in-law/son-in-law, or other close family ties.

When the essential bonding between parents and child is missed at birth, the child is left with a sense of incompleteness. This can leave him restless and searching throughout his life. Satan can easily draw such a person into false and perverse soul ties with others.

## Chapter 8 - Soul Ties

**Breaking demonic soul ties.**
Matthew 16:19 says, "And I will give you the keys of the kingdom of heaven, and whatever you bind on earth will be bound in heaven, and whatever you loose on earth will be loosed in heaven."

No matter how much sin we have been connected to through these demonic soul ties we have the power through the blood of Jesus Christ to renounce, repent, and loosen this negative energy from our soul to be set free and filled with the Holy Spirit.

**Prayer suggestions.**
1. Be led by the Holy Spirit through prayer that God will help you remember everyone you have had any sexual relations with. Ask the Lord if there were any sexual encounters in early childhood that you may have been too young to remember.

2. This is serious spiritual warfare; therefore we do not need to do this alone. We need to find a mature Christian who we trust to lead us through these prayers. This builds a healthy soul tie.

3. Repentance for the sin against God is necessary. God's ordinances have been violated. Lust has taken us beyond the boundaries of purity that the Lord set for us.

Even if the sin was committed in ignorance, it still requires forgiveness. Ask God to forgive you for each perverse soul tie that you have created.

4. Spoil the devil's house by taking back all that he has gained against you. Confess before God that Satan has no further legal right to you. Declare each demonic soul tie that you have identified to be broken in the name of the Lord Jesus Christ.

5. Command the evil spirits associated with the soul ties to leave you in the name of Jesus Christ, the Son of God.

Note. Be as specific as possible when breaking soul ties. Soul ties are formed with each person with whom you have had sexual relationship outside of marriage. Name each person and break the soul tie. Are there any soul ties with animals? Are there any unnatural soul ties with family members? Have spiritually perverse soul ties been created through homosexuality or through occult (idolatrous) involvements, such as fortune telling, hypnotism, ESP, blood covenants, unholy vows, horoscopes, etc.? Have you had an abortion or are the father of an abort child the soul tie should be broken between you and that child.

**Breaking soul ties prayer.**
Soul ties are formed between specific people; therefore, the breaking of soul ties should be with those specific people. It is the same when we are asking forgiveness for judging someone. If names cannot be brought to mind, descriptions to identify the person or the occasion should be used. Also, the more specific we can be the more specific we are able to repent, either for the soul tie, or for the judging.

Soul ties are like two pieces of particleboard glued together. When the pieces are separated, particles of each remain with the other.

**I have inordinate soul ties with**

_____

_____

_____

I break those soul ties in Jesus' name and renounce them. I ask Jesus for forgiveness for my actions that may have made the ties, and I forgive those who made soul ties to me. I take back every particle of my soul that I may have left with other people, and release every particle of any souls that may be attached to me.

**I repent of the sin(s) of** _____ in Jesus name. (Write the sin(s) in this blank)

**I break the soul tie with** _____ I take back my soul particles and I give them back theirs in Jesus name. (The person's name goes in the blank)

I repent of any anger or resentment that I may have toward you God for allowing this to happen. I ask you to forgive me.

I repent of any anger or resentment that I may have toward myself for involvement with this sin. I forgive myself.

I repent of any anger or resentment toward the other party involved in this sin. I forgive them. I command any evil spirits associated with this sin to leave in Jesus name it now under the blood of Jesus. Lord, fill me up with your Holy Spirit in these places of my soul. I thank you and I praise you, Jesus gets all the glory, Amen.

# Chapter 9
# Grieving
A step towards healing

Grieving is an involuntary and natural human reaction to loss of any kind. It is what we do with grieving that makes all the difference in our lives. We can stuff it and pretend it does not exist, or we can grieve continuously throughout our lives and stay in self-pity. Both of these responses will keep us in bondage. However, there is a healthy way to deal with grieving that will allow God to give us the freedom that He desires to give to us. Jesus died for our losses, He traded places with us, and now we need to learn how to appropriate His healing.

You need to be real with God over losses in your life. They can be regrets from your youth, perhaps people who have passed on, the loss of a spouse or child through death, divorce or rebellion, and the list goes on. People grieve over the loss of their dreams, visions and plans for their lives.

Often they get mad at God over their losses. Many people do not even recognize their pain as a loss, in which case those issues are buried deep in the soul as a wound effecting affecting their entire life.

**Mourning is grieving.**
Matthew 5:2-4 says, "Then He opened His mouth and taught them, saying: "Blessed *are* the poor in spirit, For theirs is the kingdom of heaven. Blessed *are* those who mourn, For they shall be comforted."

Mourning comes from deep in the heart, not for sinful acts, but from knowing that you are poor in spirit, repenting from trying to make it on your own, and seeing His love and grace to come to your aid.

I saw a movie that was based on a true story in an American school that dealt with young people from different inner city ghettos. The populations of these ghettos were made up of varied cultures which all came together in a high school. The 15-year-old children were members of gangs, drug users, and totally undisciplined with no interest at all in school. Violence and even murder was common. The various cultures – Blacks, Latinos, and Asians – all hated one another. On the scene came a young white teacher with a heart to change things. She struggled for some time with insolent children who hated her, but she did not give up.

The teacher tried an experiment, which makes the point about the value of grieving in the proper way. She gave each student a notebook and asked each one to keep a daily journal. They could write whatever they pleased, and were not required to show their journal to her. However, the students all voluntarily turned in their journals and wanted the teacher to read them. They wrote about their horrible childhoods, their suffering in the gang infested ghettos, the abuse from their parents, and other such things.

These children were grieving. They caught the ear of compassion and poured out their hearts. This true story was amazing. The students began to love and respect their teacher, they began to read books about other's sufferings, even the Nazi holocaust, and the different cultures began to bond and love one another. What happened? They discharged their griefs and were healed. Journaling with the Lord about your losses is powerful.

**The following are excerpts taken from the <u>Inner Healing</u> book [17] we have been using in this series.**
One of the most important things we need to learn is how to grieve. Grieving is the ability to recognize and mourn the losses we have experienced. God has given us the ability to grieve. If any of us have lost a family member through death, we may have grieved that loss.

---

[17] <u>Inner Healing</u> Copyright * 1992 by Dunklin Memorial Church – Used by permission ISOB

## Chapter 9 – Grieving

Problems arise within us when we experience losses in our lives, but do not grieve those losses. Instead of grieving, we allow ourselves to become hardened inside. As a result, we react to those things in the wrong way. We become resentful and angry about with them. We do not recognize the hurt, pain and loss, and we do not allow the Lord to minister to us in those areas.

Society has told us a lie we believe to be true. We were told that men don't cry; therefore brave little boys don't cry if they want to become men. A man should not show hurt or emotion, or pain. But that is a lie.

It becomes a major problem with us when we don't allow ourselves to express the sorrow we feel. We don't realize that if we will be open and honest with God, He will heal us in those areas of our lives. As we bring these things to the light of Christ, He is able to minister His healing to us.

Many of the things that hurt us in our lives have been jammed into the inner recesses of our minds with the hope that they will be forgotten. What we don't realize is that these things continue to affect us in our reactions to the events and the people we encounter daily. We need to learn how to be honest, how to bring out the emotions, and how to grieve about them. As we allow them to surface, God begins a process in us that gives us insight and wisdom about them. The healing can then take place.

One obstacle to our healing is that when we are hurt, we are able to see only our side of the situation. We are unable to see the situation from God's side. This means we are unable to see the whole picture, we see only one side of it.

There is one danger in grieving. We can become caught up in it and never allow ourselves to get out. If we are caught up in grieving, we become very depressed. We find ourselves filled with self-pity and self-condemnation. There is a legitimate time for grieving but there is definitely a time to move on.

I don't think that there is anybody that would turn down an offer from God to allow Him to produce in their life what His original purpose has always been for them.

## Chapter 9 – Grieving

How can we cooperate with God, what are some of the main ingredients? I submit that there are several. However, in this chapter we will cover what I believe to be the first, the most important, and the one without which we will certainly never realize God's purpose for our lives, that is being real with God.

## That ingredient is truth.
### *There are two primary aspects of truth.*

Psalm 85 says that when our truth rises up from the earth, that we receive righteousness from heaven. In other words, Jesus, the Truth, is already there, but in order to make contact, we have to "send" our truth to Him.

"Mercy and truth have met together; Righteousness and peace have kissed. Truth shall spring out of the earth, And righteousness shall look down from heaven. Yes, the LORD will give what is good; And our land will yield its increase. Righteousness will go before Him, And shall make His footsteps our pathway" (Psalm 85:10-13).

### *The first aspect of truth is to be real with yourself and God.*
### *1 John states that our truth leads to cleansing.*

"This is the message which we have heard from Him and declare to you, that God is light and in Him is no darkness at all. If we say that we have fellowship with Him, and walk in darkness, we lie and do not practice the truth. But if we walk in the light as He is in the light, we have fellowship with one another, and the blood of Jesus Christ His Son cleanses us from all sin. If we say that we have no sin, we deceive ourselves, and the truth is not in us. If we confess our sins, He is faithful and just to forgive us our sins and to cleanse us from all unrighteousness. If we say that we have not sinned, we make Him a liar, and His word is not in us" (1 John 1:5-10).

We cannot deny, nor successfully bury our actual feelings, experiences and emotions without paying a horrible price. While we are not supposed to live on our ungodly feelings, nor are we to be guided by our emotions, we do have to "give" them to God as something that really exists.

Chapter 9 – Grieving

We don't deny that feelings and emotions exist; but we do deny their right to govern our lives. We confess them to the Lord Jesus and He takes those parts of them that are not of Him, the sin, and forgives and removes them.

**The following excerpts were taken from the book <u>Be Real with God</u>.** [18]

*God's original design for your life was to be in a living relationship with Him. The purpose of this book is to help you find that relationship and walk in it. It is not to add to the layers of roles that we play in life, especially religious roles and religious play-acting. I pray that this book will encourage you to become transparent with God, your Creator, and through that transparency to experience God's wonderful love and grace which will mold you into His original design for your life.*

***Every one of us starts out as who we really are.***
***Then we develop different attitudes of who we want to be.***

*The "want to be's" become roles that we play. Quite often these decisions are made subconsciously. All of these roles build up like layers of an onion in our lives. It is God's purpose to take us back to who we really are, to the real "you." That is the "you" that God really loves and it is the only "you" that God can really work with to make you whole and fulfilled in life.*

***We fear the discovery of who we really are.***

*Over the years we have constructed layers of self-deceit upon ourselves similar to layers of an onion. We have so many ways of hiding behind roles that others or ourselves have constructed. These roles are self-deceiving and we have become so lost behind them that we are incapable of rescuing ourselves. Before we know it we are*

---

[18] Quote taken from the book Be Real with God – by Larry Chkoreff

## Chapter 9 – Grieving

*hiding behind so many layers that we are totally self-deceived and fit into what Jeremiah said, "The heart is deceitful above all things and beyond cure. Who can understand it?" (Jeremiah 17:9).*

*True contentment in life is knowing that the real you is acceptable. It is knowing that you can be real with God. It is knowing that you don't know how to be completely real in one big event, but that as you go through life, God will cause the layers to be taken off little by little as you can tolerate it and accept it. You discover that God accepts you just the way you are, however, He wants to peel back the layers to get to the real you. You will find out that God is gentle throughout this process. You will discover that quite often even the gentleness can be painful.*

*There can be hidden compartments in your life that you do not want anybody, especially God, to uncover and expose. You know it would be too painful. But God would say to you, "Go ahead and trust me to touch that hurt just one time. I may cause more pain in your life by touching it, but after that, healing will come. Is it worth it?" It is like the surgeon asking, "Is it worth it to bear the pain of my knife if it means cutting out the disease?"*

*There is a law on planet Earth that always works: it is called sowing and reaping (Galatians 6:7-8). One will ultimately reap whatsoever he sows. This law applies to truth also. If you sow the truth you will reap the truth. If you sow deception and dishonesty, you will reap darkness, and the truth will not shine in your life. "Everyone who is of the truth hears My voice" (John 18:37 b).*

*King David made the following statement in Psalm 32:2-3 after trying to hide his terrible sins from God. David could no longer live with himself, but he discovered that God honors the truth and that the truth will make one free.*

## Chapter 9 – Grieving

*"Blessed is the man whose sin the LORD does not count against him and in whose spirit is no deceit. When I kept silent, my bones wasted away through my groaning all day long" (Psalm 32:2-3). I suggest that you read the entire Psalm 32.*

*There is usually a price for being truly honest. Proverbs 23:23 says, "Buy the truth, and do not sell it, Also wisdom and instruction and understanding." One price you need to be prepared to pay is humility.*

*I believe that evil came to pass in our world and continues to exist by man's dishonesty. The cartoon below illustrates this. To the degree that you are not real, is the degree of potential evil or darkness that exists in your life. The wider the gap, the greater the potential is for evil.*

**Being real is the first aspect of truth, the second aspect of truth is Jesus.**

*His Word is the ultimate Truth. However, His Word will not be revealed to those who do not first practice the first truth, which is gut-level honesty with themselves before God.*

**Jesus called Himself "Truth."**

*"Jesus said to him, 'I am the way, the truth, and the life. No one comes to the Father except through Me'" (John 14:6).*

*The Holy Spirit's name is Truth.*

*"But when the Helper comes, whom I shall send to you from the Father, the Spirit of truth who proceeds from the Father, He will testify of Me" (John 15:26).*

*Freedom has some conditions, one of which is truth.*

*When the two aspects of truth outlined above touch each other, God can go to work. Other conditions stated below in John chapter 8 are abiding in His Word, being Jesus' disciple, obeying Him and not claiming a right to your own life. Then you will know the Truth, which is to have a relationship with Him, Truth incarnate!*

## Chapter 9 – Grieving

*"Then Jesus said to those Jews who believed Him, 'If you abide in My word, you are My disciples indeed. And you shall know the truth, and the truth shall make you free.' They answered Him, 'We are Abraham's descendants, and have never been in bondage to anyone. How can you say, 'You will be made free'?' Jesus answered them, 'Most assuredly, I say to you, whoever commits sin is a slave of sin. And a slave does not abide in the house forever, but a son abides forever. Therefore if the Son makes you free, you shall be free indeed'" (John 8:31-36).*

*You must be real about your emotions, feelings and pain in order to enable God to set you free.*

**Godly grieving.**
God set up the grieving process for us. However, if we are not cautious, we can get into un-godly grieving.

There are six stages of grief which usually manifest themselves in the following sequence, however, it is natural to move back and forth between these steps as we progress:

*1. Denial.* We simply do not want to accept the misfortune.

*2. Bargaining with God.* If God will restore or repair or replace what we are grieving about, we will do whatever He wants.

*3. Anger.* We are totally undeserving of what has happened and we feel we have been treated unfairly. This justifies our anger.

*4. Acceptance.* We accept that it happened, and we concede that we can do nothing about it.

*5. Grief of the loss.* We become honest about our feelings, share those feelings with others and allow ourselves to be healed.

*6. Resolution.* We resolve to pick up the pieces and get on with life.

**Another level of truth**
We also want to be honest about our sinful reactions to what has happened to us. There are three principles we may have violated

## Chapter 9 – Grieving

in our reactions to what people have done to us or to what life has delivered to us.

1. Judgment. We are told in scripture we are not to judge, lest we be judged.

2. Honoring our father and our mother. If we do not, our life will not go well with us.

3. Sowing and Reaping. When we plant seeds, we can expect to reap a harvest.

**The Good News!**
*Jesus bore our griefs.*

"Surely He has borne our griefs And carried our sorrows; Yet we esteemed Him stricken, Smitten by God, and afflicted" (Isaiah 53:4).

When we let out the truth of our grief, we then can reap the truth of His healing. He took our place! Jesus took the sorrows and griefs of everybody that ever lived when He died on the Cross. He took it for you that you might be free!

**Jesus' mission is to make us free people, healed on the inside and free from the sin perpetrated against us by losses.**

First notice the exchanges that Jesus came to give us, then notice the promises to those who accept His gift.

**Isaiah 61:1-11 says,**

*1 "The Spirit of the Lord GOD is upon Me, Because the LORD has anointed Me To preach good tidings to the poor; He has sent Me to heal the brokenhearted, To proclaim liberty to the captives, And the opening of the prison to those who are bound;*

*2 To proclaim the acceptable year of the LORD, And the day of vengeance of our God; To comfort all who mourn **[grieve]**,*

*3 To console those who mourn in Zion, To give them beauty for ashes, The oil of joy for mourning, The garment of praise for the spirit of heaviness; That they may be*

## Chapter 9 – Grieving

*called trees of righteousness, The planting of the LORD, that He may be glorified."*

*4 And they shall rebuild the old ruins, They shall raise up the former desolations, And they shall repair the ruined cities, The desolations of many generations.*

*5 Strangers shall stand and feed your flocks, And the sons of the foreigner Shall be your plowmen and your vinedressers.*

*6 But you shall be named the priests of the LORD, They shall call you the servants of our God. You shall eat the riches of the Gentiles, And in their glory you shall boast.*

*7 Instead of your shame you shall have double honor, And instead of confusion they shall rejoice in their portion. Therefore in their land they shall possess double; Everlasting joy shall be theirs.*

*8 "For I, the LORD, love justice; I hate robbery for burnt offering; I will direct their work in truth, And will make with them an everlasting covenant.*

*9 Their descendants shall be known among the Gentiles, And their offspring among the people. All who see them shall acknowledge them, That they are the posterity whom the LORD has blessed."*

*10 I will greatly rejoice in the LORD, My soul shall be joyful in my God; For He has clothed me with the garments of salvation, He has covered me with the robe of righteousness, As a bridegroom decks himself with ornaments, And as a bride adorns herself with her jewels.*

*11 For as the earth brings forth its bud, As the garden causes the things that are sown in it to spring forth, So the Lord GOD will cause righteousness and praise to spring forth before all the nations.*

**It is interesting to note the progression of this Isaiah 61 Scripture:**

## Chapter 9 – Grieving

1. Jesus came to help people who had losses in life, the poor, brokenhearted, captives and prisoners who were bound up with internal bondages.

2. Then He sets them free and takes vengeance on those who perpetrated the sins against those victims, that being Satan and his army.

3. After that He comforts those people. That word comfort means to have compassion to the point of causing the recipient to repent. It means that the people who were bound up see the love of God understanding them and leading them into a new life.

4. Then He consoles those who mourn in Zion. Zion represents the Kingdom of God. The word console means to appoint, ordain, teach and transform. God wants to console us after we get into Zion, the Kingdom of God. This is His method of sending out those who had previously been losers and mourners.

5. Then look at verse 61:4-11 to see the promises of what God will do with us and through us.

**A testimony.**
Just a few months after the Lord saved me in 1979 I had been "mourning" about wasting so much of my life before I found Jesus. I was telling God how I felt. I had wished that I could start over, that I was glad that I was saved, but sad about the wasted time.

I had been hungry for the Word of God and I was pursuing Pentecostal preachers since their message seemed to satisfy me more. I was receiving an audiotape each week from Church On The Way in California. Pastor Jack Hayford was preaching in a Sunday service, and he broke out in a prophetic message that was intended personally for me. I was amazed since it was on an audiotape and I was listening to it at my place of business. God was speaking directly to me.

Pastor Hayford said, in a prophetic statement, "Your life is like a scroll that had your life's plan written on it, but the scroll had been burnt around the edges. The edges of your life's scroll had turned to ashes and they fell to the ground. You cannot paste them back together to read your life's purpose. However, I am able to resurrect the ashes and put them back into your scroll so that your life's purpose can be whole again. As a matter of fact, I, the Lord, '...will restore to you the years that the swarming locust has eaten, The crawling locust, The consuming locust, And the chewing locust, My great army which I sent among you. You shall eat in plenty and be satisfied, And praise the name of the LORD your God, Who has dealt wondrously with you; And My people shall never be put to shame. Then you shall know that I *am* in the midst of Israel: I *am* the LORD your God And there is no other. My people shall never be put to shame' (Joel 2:25-27). I will make it as if there had been no wasted time in your life."

At the writing of this book, 29 years later, I can honestly say that has happened, super abundantly beyond my greatest expectations! He gave me beauty for ashes, the oil of joy for mourning.

**If you don't grieve your losses you won't have "life after death," or the miracle of resurrection in your present life.**
Notice in the Isaiah 61 Scripture that everything that is promised to us, all of the good things, are conveyed in the form of a swap or an exchange: Beauty for ashes, the oil of joy for mourning, etc. That exchange is the principle of the Cross, or in other words, the blood covenant with God. Everything we have goes to Him, and everything He has goes to us.

*This is what He received.*

"He is despised and rejected by men, A Man of sorrows and acquainted with grief. And we hid, as it were, our faces from Him; He was despised, and we did not esteem Him. Surely He has borne our griefs And carried our sorrows; Yet we esteemed Him stricken, Smitten by God, and afflicted" (Isaiah 53:3-4).

*This is the result of what He received.*

"He shall see [the fruit] of the travail of His soul and be satisfied; by His knowledge of Himself [which He possesses and imparts to others] shall My [uncompromisingly] righteous One, My Servant, justify many and make many righteous (upright and in right standing with God), for He shall bear their iniquities and their

## Chapter 9 – Grieving

guilt [with the consequences, says the Lord]" (Isaiah 53:11, Amplified Bible).

Pouring out your grieving, giving Jesus the losses in your life, will enable Him to pour out to you and through you supernatural resurrection "jewels" that could not have been produced except through your losses, your "death and resurrection."

**The following is a quote by Evelyn Akin:**

*Before we can get on with inner healing, it seems to me that we must first "reckon ye also yourselves to be dead indeed unto sin"--Rom. 6:11, which includes death to self (including and especially that part of us that harbors the hurts that we need inner healing for). Watchman Nee explains that we already "know" we died in Christ, but we must reckon it so. That means coming to the place that we not only give up our right to our very self (our right to our own life lived as we desire and control and our feelings as well), but going deeper and relinquishing our "right" to our hurts and all that has happened to us which up to this point has been WHO we are and have known ourselves to be! I would think that very often we have become what our hurts are--our identity in large measure. This means to let go of our right to react in self-pity, anger, resentment, getting even, etc. This is the true death to self, I believe. It is a willingness to say that all I've experienced can be done with never to be brought up again as if it never happened--let it be buried with Christ just my sins are buried with Him. We rejoice that our sins are taken away, but we don't also realize that the next thing is the death to self that brings us life in the Spirit but which also requires that we die to our right to our hurts.*

## Chapter 10
## Forgiveness
### The Inner Healing Ointment

We have discussed many issues regarding inner healing and wholeness in the previous chapters. However, the subject of forgiveness is *the key* element in inner healing. This is the most important issue.

Forgiveness was the death blow that defeated Satan! Unforgiveness gives Satan a license to operate in your life!

The Apostle Paul warns us in 2 Corinthians 2:10-11 about Satan taking advantage of us through unforgiveness. 2 Corinthians 2:10-11 says, "Now whom you forgive anything, I also *forgive*. For if indeed I have forgiven anything, I have forgiven that one for your sakes in the presence of Christ, lest Satan should take advantage of us; for we are not ignorant of his devices."

**I want to plant a vision in you at this point about the real meaning of forgiveness.**

Picture yourself with someone screaming at you words of insults, especially that are not true. Picture that sin going into your heart and wounding you as the Bible says it does.

Now picture Jesus stepping in between you and the perpetrator, and see that sin going into His heart instead of yours.

He "bore" our sins.

Isaiah 53:5,

"But He *was* wounded for our transgressions, *He was* bruised for our iniquities; The chastisement for our peace *was* upon Him, And by His stripes we are healed."

Isaiah 53:12-b,

"…And He bore the sin of many, And made intercession for the transgressors."

## Chapter 10- Forgiveness

When you agree with that truth you have forgiven and you are set free. He bore the sins perpetrated against you as well as the sins you have committed.

**Jesus' mission as stated in Isaiah 61, and as He spoke in Luke 4, is to set us free, through forgiveness, from the things that enslave us.**

"And He was handed the book of the prophet Isaiah. And when He had opened the book, He found the place where it was written: 'The Spirit of the LORD is upon Me, Because He has anointed Me To preach the gospel to the poor; He has sent Me to heal the brokenhearted, To proclaim liberty to the captives And recovery of sight to the blind, To set at liberty those who are oppressed; To proclaim the acceptable year of the LORD.' Then He closed the book, and gave it back to the attendant and sat down. And the eyes of all who were in the synagogue were fixed on Him. And He began to say to them, 'Today this Scripture is fulfilled in your hearing'" (Luke 4:17-21).

The acceptable year of the Lord referred to the Year of Jubilee as described in Leviticus chapter 25. This was the Sabbath of Sabbaths. The Sabbath year was every seventh year during which time people were to allow their land to rest. However, each $50^{th}$ year was the Year of Jubilee. This is when all slaves were set free and all mortgaged land and loans were forgiven. In short, this was the "Year of total forgiveness," and Jesus was proclaiming the final fulfillment of this promise in Him. This Year of Jubilee began on the Day of Atonement, which was the one day each year that the priest went into the Holy of Holies with the blood for the atonement and forgiveness of sins.

**Forgiveness is the surgery that removes our sins.**
*It is the major step towards healing.*

It is much like physical surgery. The word forgive means to remove. Its root word is death, which means to separate.

*Humans attempt to medicate their inner wounds with "outer ointments."*

The problem is that we do not even realize that our outer issues are usually the result of inner wounds, so we try all sorts of medications and activities, none of which work, indeed they make things worse. Forgiveness, as we wrote about in Chapter 1 of this book, is the ointment for inner healing.

Inner healing usually brings healing and prosperity to those "external issues" that we are so concerned with. 3 John 1:2 says, "Beloved, I pray that you may prosper in all things and be in health, just as your soul prospers."

Most inner wounds are caused by shame, rejection, lack of love and primarily broken relationships, especially with father figures. God created us for relationships and to the degree our prime relationships have been less than perfect, which includes all of us, to that same degree we acquire inner wounds. Forgiveness is the process that God created to transfer those wounds to Jesus.

## What exactly is forgiveness?

Too many people, even Christians, have misunderstood forgiveness, thus they have been kept in bondage. To forgive is to release from judgment and to give up the right to get even. When we do not release others from our judgment and give up our right to get even, we place ourselves in the position of the man in the story in Matthew 18 (below) who was unwilling to cancel the debt of his fellow slave.

If you do not agree and appropriate God's forgiveness, then you will not only be miserable, but you will also reap a horrible judgment. We reap the horrible consequences of unjust judgment we put on others. Holding on to unforgiveness is the same as judgment. Being forgiven is the opposite of judgment.

Forgiveness has nothing to do with feelings. It is entirely dependent upon our will. If we wait until we "feel" like forgiving, we will never forgive. This is especially true in situations where the wounds another person has caused are deep. The decision to forgive is made with our will, and we submit our feelings to God. He will change our feelings in due time.

## Chapter 10- Forgiveness

**Forgiveness runs in two directions.**
*It is for the sins we have committed, and for the sins committed against us.*

It is not excusing someone or someone's sin. It does not excuse sin. In order to forgive one must admit that a terrible wrong has been done. Neither does forgiveness carry a demand to go back into an abusive situation to be abused, controlled, or manipulated by another.

Most people understand that they need to be forgiven when they sin, but often do not completely understand what forgiving others is about. Jesus stood between you and the person who perpetrated sin against you. Jesus bore your sin. All you have to do is agree, and you will be set free.

**Forgive means to separate.**
It is the same word used in the New Testament for death. To die is to be separated. To forgive requires cutting the sin away from one and putting on another.

*Forgiveness defined*: (Greek) aphiemi - means to remove – to send away, to remove, the remission for the punishment due to sinful conduct, the deliverance of the sinner from the penalty.

To forgive someone means to account their sin against you as having been done, not to you, but to Jesus, and to agree to allow the sin and its penalty to rest there and there alone!

**Forgiveness is a finished work of Jesus.**
All we have to do is believe the truth, that all sin has already been put on Jesus. When we agree that the work has been done, then our part of the transaction has been completed, and we are set free. It is not so much in our doing, but more in our believing and in taking the corresponding action in what we believe. John 1:29 says, "The next day John saw Jesus coming toward him, and said, 'Behold! The Lamb of God who takes away the sin of the world!'"

**Jesus gave us a clear message and a warning in Matthew 18.**
    **Matthew 18:21-35 says,**

## Chapter 10- Forgiveness

*21 Then Peter came to Him and said, "Lord, how often shall my brother sin against me, and I forgive him? Up to seven times?"*

*22 Jesus said to him, "I do not say to you, up to seven times, but up to seventy times seven.*

*23 "Therefore the kingdom of heaven is like a certain king who wanted to settle accounts with his servants.*

*24 "And when he had begun to settle accounts, one was brought to him who owed him ten thousand talents.*

*25 "But as he was not able to pay, his master commanded that he be sold, with his wife and children and all that he had, and that payment be made.*

*26 "The servant therefore fell down before him, saying, 'Master, have patience with me, and I will pay you all.'*

*27 "Then the master of that servant was moved with compassion, released him, and forgave him the debt.*

*28 "But that servant went out and found one of his fellow servants who owed him a hundred denarii; and he laid hands on him and took him by the throat, saying, 'Pay me what you owe!'*

*29 "So his fellow servant fell down at his feet and begged him, saying, 'Have patience with me, and I will pay you all.'*

*30 "And he would not, but went and threw him into prison till he should pay the debt.*

*31 "So when his fellow servants saw what had been done, they were very grieved, and came and told their master all that had been done.*

*32 "Then his master, after he had called him, said to him, 'You wicked servant! I forgave you all that debt because you begged me.*

*33 'Should you not also have had compassion on your fellow servant, just as I had pity on you?'*

*34 "And his master was angry, and delivered him to the torturers [Greek: basanistes, inferring the jailers by definition] until he should pay all that was due to him.*

## Chapter 10- Forgiveness

*35 "So My heavenly Father also will do to you if each of you, from his heart, does not forgive his brother his trespasses."*

### In this parable the Master forgives, but the servant refuses.
It is obvious that the servant does not believe that he has been forgiven. A debtless man has no need to collect money. A freed man has no need to bribe his way of escape. It would be natural for a man who has been released a great debt to dance the whole way home, anxious to tell his family of their new found freedom, and ready to help others with similar liabilities. This servant either questioned the Master's mercy, or doubted his own safety, or denied his own ability to be forgiven. Only after we accept forgiveness for ourselves are we able to forgive others. When we refuse to forgive we are the ones who suffer as a result!

### We always pay the penalty for the sin we do not forgive in others.
Notice the wicked servant did not have to pay his original and forgiven debt, described in verse 25, but had to pay the debt of the man he did not forgive, as in verse 34.

You get what you don't forgive, memories, thoughts, deeds, you will experience here and/or in eternity. This is a spiritual law. Notice the penalty was to be delivered to the torturers or tormentors, which means the jailers. Unforgiveness will always result in torment. The torturers that we are handed over to include anger, fear, guilt, resentment, hatred, bitterness, shame, etc. When we walk in unforgiveness our families and loved ones are also affected just as the slave's wife and children in this teaching.

### What gives you the right to refuse to forgive?
"I have been crucified with Christ; it is no longer I who live, but Christ lives in me; and the *life* which I now live in the flesh I live by faith in the Son of God, who loved me and gave Himself for me" (Galatians 2:20).

## Chapter 10- Forgiveness

If, as the Scripture verifies, you have indeed been crucified with Christ, and He now lives in you; then who are you to keep Him from forgiving? His very essence is forgiving. That is who He is! If you do not forgive you are denying Him. It is a very serious matter.

If we find ourselves in that position with a wicked heart, we can get rid of it with 1 John 1:9 which says "If we confess (agree with God's judgment) our sins, He is faithful and just to forgive us our sins (take them away from us and put them on Jesus) and cleanse us from ALL unrighteousness."

God gave us the gift of some warning signs to help us avoid the horrible consequence of unforgiveness. Most people would not view hatred and anger as a warning sign, but they are. Also, if you find yourself continually talking about an offense done to you or a past wound, that could be a good indicator that you are not finished with forgiveness with that matter.

If you ever sense these warnings in your life, quickly seek God about some sort of forgiveness issue. Some more advanced warning signs could be some form of torment, spiritual, emotional and even physical. It is clear from the Matthew 18 story that one of the results of unforgiveness is torment.

**A testimony.**
Ever since I met the Lord I have been quick to decide to forgive. However, it has not always been easy. There have been times when I have had to "mourn" over a wrong done to me, and just forgive by a violent act of my will. I do not have the natural disposition to ignore lies said about me, therefore that has been my greatest trial in forgiveness. There have been times when I went through a process of forgiveness for years before I actually could "feel" the victory. I can remember times of total victory after I just agonized with the Lord about forgiving certain people. One time I had been agonizing with my emotions for months about forgiving a person. I had forgiven as an act of my will, and had spoken it aloud dozens of times, but my emotions were fighting me. As I was traveling one day, I stopped at a restaurant off the highway for

a snack. Suddenly I realized that I was just within a few miles of where this person lived. I felt the Holy Spirit working on me, and that morning my inner being finally was set free. Later this person came to me with a written apology.

**Forgive yourself**
*The following is a quote from* ***Reaching Towards The Heights*** *by Richard Wurmbrand.* [19]

"Forgetting those things which are behind." (Philippians 3:13)

Shema Israel, Adonai, Eloheinu, Adonai, ehad.

"Listen Israel, the Lord your God is one God." It was this prayer (the words above are their Hebrew original) that was on the lips of many Jews who went to Eichmann's gas chambers while he looked on smiling.

Some twenty years later he was captured by the Israeli Secret Police in Buenos Aires. In his provisional prison, he amazed the guards by reciting this same prayer; this was even more amazing since he claimed not to be a believer at all.

I have known well the world of murderers and big criminals. A mysterious identification with their victims happens in their souls. Mass murderers of Jews became much more obsessed with Jewishness than any Jew would be. Professional abortionists will be haunted by a world of children who point at them, putting the question, "Why did you kill me?" The man who dropped the atomic bomb on Hiroshima, when asked by reporters, "How do you feel about it?" answered, "How did they feel about it?"

We have many victims in life. Jesus became the ideal victim, the innocent lamb betrayed, insulted, wronged, killed for our misdoings. And He died with the words, "Father, forgive them, for they know not what they do."

---

[19] Richard Wurmbrand – *Reaching For Toward The Heights*. Living Sacrifice Book Company. Bartlesville, OK., 1979, pages 221-223.

*Then He addresses Himself to us and says, "I, the victim, have forgiven you. All your victims are now in a world where forgiveness reigns. You are the only one who does not forgive yourself. You are haunted by what you have done. Accept forgiveness. Forgive yourself. The unhealthy identification with the men whom you have wronged will cease. You will have a new personality.*

Define forgiveness as death. Forgiveness is the death of sin, sin goes into another realm away from you onto Jesus.

**Remember who you are!**
You are a vessel filled with God, the Temple of God.
   ***Prayer.***
   Jesus, I, by an act of my will and my words, acknowledge that the sin perpetrated against me by others was actually borne by You. You took it, not me. Therefore I am free from the affects of that sin against me.
   I also, as an act of my will and my words, acknowledge and confess my sin to You, Lord. Your Word says that when I confess my sin You are faithful and just to forgive me and to cleanse me of all unrighteousness (1 John 1:9).

**Dunklin quotes the following from the book Inner Healing.**
   *FORGIVENESS IS NOT:*
   *1. Overlooking the wrong done to us.*
   *We like to believe that if we overlook a wrong done to us, it will go away. In reality it does not. Overlooking something is not forgiveness; it is a form of repression or denial.*
   *Some of us were hurt by what people said or did as we were growing up, and we tried to overlook those things. But the truth is, they had a great effect upon our lives. Repressing and overlooking offenses does not mean we have forgiven. If there is still pain inside, it is a sign there is probably unforgiveness still inside.*

*2. Excusing or whitewashing the wrong done to us.*

When we try to make excuses or water down an offense, we are actually trying to tell ourselves that it really wasn't as bad as it seemed. This is justifying or rationalizing, but it is not forgiveness.

*3. Psycho-analyzing a person's nature to explain why he did the wrong to us.*

It is important that we understand exactly what happened, but understanding and forgiveness are two different things. While Jesus was hanging on the cross, He said, Forgive them for they know not what they do. As we come out of chemical addiction, we may be able to analyze our actions, but we really can't explain them away.

Knowing what has motivated a person to behave the way he has will help us forgive that person. But knowing is not the same as forgiving. We can know about a person, and we can even know why he behaved the way he did, but still not forgive him. Understanding a person's behavior doesn't mean we have forgiven him.

Sin is moral stupidity, it is unexplainable. The Apostle Paul said, The things I do I do not understand. (Romans 7:15) So we must know that we don't base our forgiveness upon understanding. That means we don't have to understand in order to forgive.

Some people spend years in self-help and therapy groups, trying to analyze their childhood and understand why their parents mistreated them. They are often disillusioned to find they are no better off after their efforts than before they started. Forgiveness is the key that unlocks us from the binding judgments we formed in our painful past.

We have to look at ourselves before we can experience healing. It is possible for us to say, "I understand why my father acted the way he did. I understand where he was coming from, but I just can't forgive him."

## Chapter 10- Forgiveness

*If we are unwilling to get beyond our feelings and make a decision to forgive, we will never be able to receive God's healing in our lives. We may finally understand the reason for a person's behavior, but if we don't have the will to forgive, there will be no forgiveness for either party.*

*4. Taking the blame for the wrong done to us.*

*This happens often in child abuse. Taking the blame is not the same thing as forgiveness. It is proper for us to take the blame for our reaction to the experience. But if we were physically, mentally or sexually abused as a child, it was not our fault. If we take the blame for it, that is not forgiveness.*

*Many of those who have been sexually abused have the blame imposed upon them. Many young victims are told it was their fault, that they had a part in it. If they are convinced it was their fault and they take the blame that is still not the same as forgiveness. It may create the feeling of forgiveness toward the abuser, but that is only because the anger has been turned inward.*

*All the above reactions are improper attitudes, which reflect internal problems and misunderstandings. We short-circuit what God wants to accomplish in us if we attempt to substitute any of these attitudes for forgiveness.*

*FORGIVENESS IS:*
*1. Facing the specific wrong done to us.*

*We can neither excuse it nor rationalize it. We have to be honest. Listed below are six words. Taking each word independently, close your eyes and picture in your mind specific events related to them.*

*a) Rejection.*

*Picture events in which you may have felt the need for love and acceptance, but it was withheld from you; you wanted attention, but you were ignored.*

*b) Neglect.*

## Chapter 10- Forgiveness

*A typical example of neglect in an alcoholic family is when the parents spend money on liquor instead of purchasing food or other essentials.*

*c) Injustice or unfairness.*

*This is when the punishment doesn't fit the crime. You may never have known whether you were going to be hugged or slugged. It also may have been difficult for you to figure out what brought on the different reactions.*

*d) Cruelty or brutality.*

*This could have been either physical or verbal. Verbal cruelty always identified you with your actions. For example, you were not told you did something stupid, you were told you were stupid because of what you did.*

Chapter 10- Forgiveness

**Forgiveness Worksheet**

List the people who have caused pain in your life.

List the people who you have had a difficult time forgiving.

Write in your own words, from your own feelings, how you feel about these people. Be honest, do not pretend.

Now as an act of your will, not from your feelings, say, "I forgive _____. I choose to see the sin they perpetrated against me as going on to Jesus as He was my sin-bearer. Now Father I ask you to line up my feelings with my decision to forgive." " But if you do not forgive men their trespasses, neither will your Father forgive your trespasses" (Matthew 6:15).

Now list the sins that you have in your life. Confess them to the Lord. Confess means to speak, but also to agree with how Jesus sees them.
    "If we confess our sins, He is faithful and just to forgive us *our* sins and to cleanse us from all unrighteousness" (1 John 1:9).

**This Father will never leave you!**
"For He Himself has said, 'I will never leave you nor forsake you'" (Hebrews 13:5b). You never have to fear again. Your conduct will not be perfect; you will still sin from time to time. Even then, your Father will never leave you nor forsake you. He will always be there to turn you around and bring you back. He is passionate about you.

Now take this sheet of paper, and nail it to a piece of wood, as if it were the Cross of Jesus. After that remove it from the cross and burn it as a symbol of it being totally consumed.

## Chapter 11
## Scab And Scars

In our previous chapter on forgiveness we wrote about how forgiveness removes our sins, and thus heals our wounds. However, we have learned that our wounds are not truly removed but rather they are converted from scabs to scars. It is interesting to note that even Jesus kept His scars. John 20:27 (Amplified Bible) says, "Then He said to Thomas, Reach out your finger here, and see My hands; and put out your hand and place [it] in My side. Do not be faithless and incredulous, but [stop your unbelief and] believe!"

Scabs are the covering over a wound with dried blood. They can be easily opened again when picked at. Scars are the evidence where a wound once was, but is no longer subject to pain. Scars do not relay pain when touched. However, later in this chapter you will see how God's power works to turn those scabs into scars.

**The following is a quote from <u>Inner Healing</u>, by Dunklin.** [20]

*Romans 12:2 says, "And do not be conformed to this world, but be transformed by the renewing of your mind, that you may prove what is that good and acceptable and perfect will of God."*

*In regard to renewing the mind, we have had many opportunities during this study to forgive everyone who has caused us harm during our lifetime. This is a giant step in the process of renewal. Now it is time to see how well we have done in the area of forgiveness.*

*Perhaps we have been told that unless we are able to forget, we really haven't forgiven, but that is simply untrue.*

*For example, everyone probably has scars that have healed. We all have scars we can point to. We experienced some sort of physical mishap, which caused an abrasion in*

---

[20] Copyright * 1992 by Dunklin Memorial Church – Used by permission ISOB

## Chapter 11 – Scabs and Scars

*our skin. It probably bled for a while, and then it scabbed over. Finally, it healed.*

*After it healed, it became a scar. Now, as we relive that experience, we can still remember it well, but we do not feel any of the hurt. We can remember it and point to it, but we no longer feel the pain.*

*Is such a thing possible emotionally as well as physically? Is it possible that we might be able to remember a past hurt, yet not feel the hurt in the present? It is time for us to understand that although we have been hurt inside, and we have suffered because of the emotional things that have happened to us, it isn't necessary for us to forget those things. Forgetting is not necessarily a part of the healing process.*

*As a matter of fact, Jesus Christ would have us <u>not</u> forget those things. He wants to heal our hurts and let them become scars, which we can point to for His glory. There is nothing wrong in having a scar. As a matter of fact, a scar can be a plus. We need to get beyond the scars and begin thinking about how Jesus is going to lead us from this point onward. We can look at the incidents in our lives that hurt us, allow Jesus to heal the hurts, then use those incidents to His glory.*

*It is important for us to discover our purpose in life. It may never have occurred to us that one of the purposes in our lives is to utilize the scars in our lives to His glory. Imagine what it would be like to be able to point to an emotional scar and tell a hurting person, "I know what you are going through, because I have experienced that hurt. That happened to me also.*

*But look here, it has healed. I can tell you the details, I can tell you everything that happened, I can remember word for word what happened. But you see, I don't feel the pain any more, because it is healed. God healed it in me; therefore, He can heal it in you."*

## Chapter 11 – Scabs and Scars

*Every one of us has at least one incident, and some of us have many incidents in our lives, which have been traumatic to us. We now have a choice while we are in this program. Our choice is, if our hurt has not been healed yet, what are we going to do about it?*

*There is one sure way in which we can tell whether or not we have forgiven someone: When we talk about it, when we share it, are we picking at a scab, or are we pointing at a scar? We can pick at the scab, and it will never heal. We can continue to pick at the scab, and continue, and continue, and it will continue to bleed, and continue to hurt, and continue to fester, and continue to poison us.*

*We may even deliberately pick at it to make it bleed some more. We may even want to feel the pain again. It may have become a way for us to manipulate others, or to receive sympathy from someone.*

*The alternative is to give the hurt to God and allow Him to heal it. We can let it become a scar, so we will be able to point to it, and say, "God healed this. I know what you're going through, I went through the same thing. But God healed it. Let me tell you about it, because He can heal you, too."*

*It becomes obvious that we have to begin to think beyond where we are this moment. We have to think beyond the suffering we may be feeling right now. We can get ourselves beyond that, because God has another purpose for us.*

*We have to move into a scar status in order to reach the fulfillment of God's plan, because the scabs will stand in our way to God's purpose. The reason is that the scabs will always influence our responses and our reactions to everything that occurs in our lives. So long as our wounds are still bleeding, so long as we are still picking at them, subconsciously they have an effect upon our response to everything that is said to us. Every situation that occurs in*

### Chapter 11 – Scabs and Scars

*our lives will be filtered through our emotional scabs, until those scabs have been healed.*

Think about it. What if every day we would keep knocking or picking those scabs loose, and we would be bleeding all over everything? Wouldn't that be a mess? That would be our condition if we had not pressed into forgiveness for all the issues in our lives. When we allow it to scar over this brings healing and wholeness. The only way to overcome the world is to overcome the world in ourselves. However, we can't forget about the bondage that God has rescued us from. Forgetting is not part of our healing. By continuing the lifestyle of inner healing we not only establish our own success but we begin assisting others. Christ's definition of success, in addition to forgiveness and freedom, is to give the life that we have freely received away to others.

2 Corinthians 1:3-4 says, "Blessed *be* the God and Father of our Lord Jesus Christ, the Father of mercies and God of all comfort, who comforts us in all our tribulation, that we may be able to comfort those who are in any trouble, with the comfort with which we ourselves are comforted by God."

**A testimony.**
In the previous chapter about forgiveness, I gave a short testimony about agonizing with the Lord about some difficult forgiveness issues. Now I have victory over those difficult issues, however, I have not forgotten them. To my surprise, now when I remember those people and those incidents, I actually praise God for the experiences. I see now how these painful experiences not only helped to develop character in my life, but also helped to thrust me into the perfect path and will of God for my life. Therefore, now when I recall those painful times when people hurt me, there is no more pain. I actually thank God for them because they have helped me so much. They are scars. I now have a very close and sweet relationship with that individual who I had trouble forgiving. They have actually worked for my advantage; just as the scars on Jesus worked out God's perfect will for you and for me.

## Chapter 11 – Scabs and Scars

**Scabs and scars are also caused by difficult life circumstances.**
Whether or not you have decided to live under the Lordship of Jesus, you will inevitably encounter difficult, if not seemly impossible, challenges in your life. It may be financial, relational, health, marriage, or some other issue. The reasons for this are many and varied. Hopefully these types of difficulties bring us into a more dependent relationship with the Lord, and through spiritual warfare, bring God's purposes and promises into our lives. They tend to burn off our old flesh nature and mature us into the image of Christ.

How we respond to these difficulties has a great affect on our lives. Some people get mad at God for allowing them to happen. Some blame other people or even institutions for their hard times. For example, many people blame their national governments for their financial difficulties. People can blame others for marriage breakups, for children rebelling, and other such things.

Blame will keep you in bondage and will cause wounds to occur which remain as scabs. There is really no one to forgive; therefore it is difficult to become free. Oddly enough, even a perceived wrong can cause a wound. In God's eyes it does not matter who is responsible. He desires to show His power working through you to overcome without blame.

There are three ways we can emerge from trials and sufferings. We can have a hard heart, one that just wants nothing more to do with walking with the Lord. We can develop a broken heart, one that always carries the victim mentality and never gets healed. Being a victim for life is satisfying to many people. Or we can develop a tender heart. A tender heart has been worked over by circumstances and the Lord, and has emerged with faith in turning all difficulties into blessings.

The solution is to make sure that your relationship with the Lord is alive, current and in good condition. If you are in touch with Him through the Holy Spirit, then He will walk you through life's difficulties with promise.

## Chapter 11 – Scabs and Scars

**God's resurrection power can convert all those bad things done to you into a blessing.** All things work together for good because of Jesus' resurrection power in us.

Romans 8:28 says, "And we know that all things work together for good to those who love God, to those who are the called according to His purpose."

In Romans 8:36 Paul quoted Psalms 44:22-23 which says.

"22 Yet for Your sake we are killed all day long; We are accounted as sheep for the slaughter.

23 Awake! Why do You sleep, O Lord? Arise! Do not cast *us* off forever."

**Notice, the writer was begging God for help.**

But in Romans 8:36 he said in all these things we are conquerors. That is because of the resurrection power of God living in us. Next, verse 8:37 says that is also because of his love.

Romans 8:36, 37 says,

"36 As it is written: "For Your sake we are killed all day long; We are accounted as sheep for the slaughter."

**37 Yet in all these things we are more than conquerors through Him who loved us."**

**Pain can be profitable.**
I can honestly say that I am now very thankful for every one of my many severe trials. I can see the profit from them. Through them God's promises have been brought into my life. These promises have resulted in supernatural blessings that would not have been possible without the suffering.

**The mystery of the Cross!**
God does not delete our past memories. He heals them through forgiveness. Why? So that we can point to them and show His glory. What glory? The wonderful miracle working work of His Cross and resurrection. Crucifying Jesus on the Cross was the most horrible crime that ever occurred against a human being. It was the most unjustified act against an innocent person. However,

look how it turned into a powerful tool through forgiveness. Jesus does not forget the Cross, but now when He thinks back on it, He sees its value. Without that horrible act perpetrated against Him and His miraculous resurrection, you and I would not be saved today.

Colossians 1:20 says, "and by Him to *reconcile* [makes friends of] all things to Himself, by Him, whether things on earth or things in heaven, having made peace through the blood of His cross." What a wonderful thought! All things, no matter how horrible, are made a friend through the Cross of Jesus.

Romans 16:25 says, "Now to Him who is able to establish you according to my gospel and the preaching of Jesus Christ, according to the revelation of the *mystery* kept secret since the world began."

Eleanor Roosevelt said, "You are no one's victim without your permission." That wasn't true when we were children, but it is true now. We no longer have to be the victims we were as children, unless we give those wounds permission, unless we insist upon picking at the scabs.

# Chapter 12
## Shame – Guilt
It's all about your identity

We have all heard about guilt. Most Christians have heard that guilt is not something that is healthy, but so many still struggle with it. Guilt just kind of hangs on to them. Is there a healthy guilt? Is there an unhealthy or a false guilt? The answer is yes to both. What some call "false guilt" can actually be shame.

**What is guilt?**
The Vine's dictionary defines guilty as:
*Enochos:* "held in, bound by, liable to a charge or actions at law, brought to trial, under judgment."

Guilty and enochos are also translated in the Greek as "danger." "Held in contained to have bound under obligation to, liable to, subject to, connecting a person to his crime." The main verb is defined as; bound, bondage like one who cannot even obtain bail during the trial, imprisoned.

God did not make a mistake when it comes to guilt. Guilt comes from what we did wrong, breaking rules or laws. Guilt does not condemn us as bad people it only convicts us that what we did was wrong. It is designed to react to God's laws and make us feel like we need help when we fall short. When we break a law, we are supposed to feel guilt so that we may come to Jesus and be cleansed. God set us up with the law in our hearts, Adam lost it, Jesus got it back. If we break the law, we are set up to feel guilty. We broke the law, and the judge and court tells us "guilty."

"For whoever shall keep the whole law, and yet stumble in one point, he is guilty of all" (James 2:10).

Under the Hebrew covenant, guilt was supposed to bring the people to the Day of Atonement with joy so that their sins would be blotted out. This had to do with the blood sacrifice that died in their place as they watched the priests kill the heifers, the goats and the other animals.

## Chapter 12 – Shame – Guilt – It's all about your identity

**How and where does guilt operate?**
Our soul has three functions: the will (volition), the mind or intellect, and the emotions. In much the same way our spirit has three functions, those being conscience, intuition, and communion (with God or the spiritual world).

"I tell the truth in Christ, I am not lying, my *conscience* also bearing me witness in the Holy Spirit" (Romans 9:1).

Guilt works on our spirit functions, it causes callousness of the three functions, and they set up like concrete and become hard. 1 Timothy 4:2 says, "Speaking lies in hypocrisy; having their conscience seared with a hot iron."

Titus 1:15 (KJV) says, "Unto the pure all things *are* pure: but unto them that are defiled and unbelieving *is* nothing pure; but even their mind and conscience is defiled."

**Many people become stuck in their past guilt.**
If you do not forgive yourself, or in other words, truly receive and realize God's forgiveness for your past sins, you will be a prisoner with horrible consequences for the rest of your life. Either Jesus' work on the Cross, His blood, was sufficient for all your past sins, or it was not. There is no in-between. You cannot help to pay for your past sins by beating yourself up with some pseudo guilt. Jesus did the work; if you have repented you are forgiven, nothing more can be done.

Some of the results of not accepting Jesus' complete blood sacrifice are that you may become judgmental of others, you will not be able to fellowship with God in the fullness of the Holy Spirit and intimacy, you will never enter into your calling in life, you will not be able to love others, others will not "like" you, your life will feel paralyzed, you may experience poor physical health, and your emotional and spiritual health will be greatly compromised. Even secular psychiatrists agree that the common denominator for psychiatric problems is guilt.

## Chapter 12 – Shame – Guilt – It's all about your identity

The Word of God says that God has forgiven you, no matter how horrible your past sins were. You are in disagreement with God if you do not receive this wonderful gift. I understand that it may seem too good to be true, however, God loves to give you things that are seemingly too good to be true!

### What is shame?
Guilt, as designed by God, is supposed to convict your conscience about sin and bring you to repentance so that your close intimacy with God is restored. Guilt does not attack the person, just what the person has done. Shame attacks your very identity and gives you the message that you are simply no good, not worthy, bad beyond repair, and in a hopeless state.

***Shame is disguised as guilt. It is a counterfeit of guilt perpetrated by Satan.***

Evil people and satanic beings have learned how to use guilt and shame against us. If Satan cannot stop us from coming to Jesus to obtain forgiveness for those things that we did wrong, then the next tool he will use is shame.

***People use shame to manipulate.***

My wife and I have both seen this in action. Satan, evil people and demons perpetrate shame and cause us to believe that we are unworthy.

Shame builds a horrible wall between God and us just as does guilt. We cannot have intimacy with Him, our conscience feels condemned and our intuition is put out of order. We feel separated from God and He cannot minister to us. We cannot sense His presence, we do not believe the Word, and we think we are unworthy good-for-nothing sinners. We are paralyzed.

Pastor Jack Hayford, of Church on the Way in Van Nuys, California, told a story of a lady who desperately was seeking the baptism in the Holy Spirit but could not seem to break through. When he ministered to her for the cleansing of shame, she immediately began to praise God in tongues.

***Shame blocks intimacy in marriage.***

## Chapter 12 – Shame – Guilt – It's all about your identity

Not only does shame block intimacy with God but it blocks it with others as well; the most important being intimacy in marriage.

**Some of the attributes of shame.**

Shame is difficult to resolve, because it is based on how you view yourself, who you believe you are. Shame is the result of not meeting the expectations or approval of others, or being looked down upon by others.

Shame says, "Don't talk, and don't tell anybody, you can't be honest." That gives you a painful internal feeling. Shame tells you that you are useless, inadequate, worthless, valueless, dirty, never good enough, no good, bad, alienated, abandoned, damaged, different, defective, alone, or dumb.

I have often wondered why so many people cannot be honest and cannot express themselves. I sense that perhaps a lot of it comes from a learned behavior of keeping "shameful things hidden."

**Shame is about who we believe we are, not about what we have done.**

Shame is a belief about yourself that there is something inherently wrong. You feel like you are hopelessly flawed.

**Shame brings self-hatred.**

People put shame on us beginning in early childhood, sometimes on purpose, sometimes innocently. Have you ever heard these shame statements?

*Shame on you*
*Do not get upset*
*Don't cry*
*Be good*
*Be nice*
*Be a man, act like a lady*
*Avoid conflict at all costs*
*You are doing that same old thing again. Won't you ever change?*
*You cannot afford to be honest*
*Act like a nice girl*
*Don't betray the family*

## Chapter 12 – Shame – Guilt – It's all about your identity

*Be seen and not heard*
*You did that after all I have done for you?*
*You make me sick*

One of the biggest avenues of shame is a fatherless home. If a child sees other children interacting with their fathers who are engaged in their lives, they might say to themselves, "I must not be good enough. What did I do wrong? Why can't I be like the other kids?" This brings a deep-rooted level of shame.

**Shame can be transmitted by abuse.**
The abuse does not even need to have been a sexual or physical abuse; simple emotional abuse will bring shame. Somehow the perpetrator steals the moral authority of the victim. The victim then takes on the responsibility for what has occurred.

*Sexual promiscuity will bring guilt and shame.* Quite often this is a subconscious issue.

*Shame can be transmitted by family patterns.*
One can learn how to manipulate people with shame because they were manipulated or because they learned the behavior from their parents.

*Some people are experts at manipulating with shame and/or guilt.*
They do it unconsciously. They just seem like they put out some sort of "spiritual powder" that fills the air with "Can't you see how bad off I am?" or, "Do you see how I have been done wrong? Or "Please feel sorry for me." Before you know it you become their slave, serving them out of their own self-pity, doing things on their behalf that you should not be doing.

Queen Victoria, queen of England during the 1800s, studied the subject of how people controlled others. She concluded that people with evil hearts know how to manipulate people with good hearts with guilt and shame.

**What do guilt and shame do if not dealt with?**
If it is not dealt with according to God's plan, guilt and shame build a wall and block your contact with God. It is difficult to hear

## Chapter 12 – Shame – Guilt – It's all about your identity

Him speak. It is difficult to pray, the Word seems lifeless. If you read the Word all you feel is condemnation.

*Guilt numbs our conscience, intuition, and communion.*

If we are going to be overcomers, we must continually hear God speak, we must have that sweet communion with Him. Otherwise we cannot know who we really are in Christ, we cannot walk a godly life, and we cannot stand against the devil.

"Healthy" guilt should drive us to repentance and to Jesus because we see our need for the blood sacrifice and for His justification. 2 Corinthians 7:10 says, "For godly sorrow produces repentance leading to salvation, not to be regretted; but the sorrow of the world produces death." The sorrow of the world is sorrow due to shame, and the end of sorrow due to shame is death, or in other words, separation from God. Death always means some type of separation.

Guilt and shame feel like a stain in your soul and spirit, and often you can even feel it in your body. Adam experienced guilt when He disobeyed God's Word.

*The cure for shame is self-forgiveness.*

When we do not forgive ourselves for bad things in our past, we keep shame pasted on ourselves. We do not respect nor love ourselves, therefore we cannot respect and love others. By not forgiving ourselves, we are claiming to be smarter than God who took all our sin and forgave us completely. The cure is to believe the truth and release the deception in our thinking.

## Good news for "bad" people. We have been justified!

Romans 5:9 says, "Much more then, having now been justified by His blood, we shall be saved from wrath through Him." Justified is a term used in courtrooms. It is the opposite of the guilt verdict. Jesus took your guilt and shame and set you free from your "jail sentence."

Isaiah 53:11 says, "He shall see the labor of His soul, and be satisfied. By His knowledge My righteous Servant shall justify [make free from guilt and shame] many, For He shall bear their iniquities."

## Chapter 12 – Shame – Guilt – It's all about your identity

Even though Jesus has justified us, we cannot stand during our trials if we are under guilt or shame. Satan attempts to keep us in guilt and/or shame so that we will not finish the process of bearing fruit and standing on the Word of God. Our job is to conduct spiritual warfare through confessing the appropriate Scriptures and continuing in the mind renewing process.

***Justification by the blood of Jesus will cleanse your conscience.***

The good news of the Gospel is meant to set us free from guilt and shame so that we may fellowship with Jesus. Being in His presence and in His Word is the only way that He can clean us up. Sure we all have areas where we still are law-breakers in one way or another, but instead of condemning us, Jesus wants us to come to Him so that He may eliminate our "flesh behavior" and reveal His character in us. Jesus calls us into His Light as He did the woman in John chapter 8 who was taken in adultery. John 8:11-12 says, "She said, 'No one, Lord.' And Jesus said to her, 'Neither do I condemn you; go and sin no more.' Then Jesus spoke to them again, saying, 'I am the light of the world. He who follows Me shall not walk in darkness, but have the light of life.'"

Our Pastor Emeritus of Mount Paran North Church of God, Dr. Paul Walker, always used the ministry style of showing his people that God does not condemn them. He emphasized the Good News. He knew that if he could remove their guilt and shame that they could connect with God for themselves and that Jesus would finish the work in that person's life. That cannot happen if you paralyzed by guilt or shame. If it is guilt then simply repent, confess your sins, ask God to help you to hate your sins, and He will cleanse you and forgive you. You will then be free to sense His presence and move on to maturity.

***Jesus offered Himself to be shamed for you and for me so that we could be free.***

Hebrews 12:2 says that Jesus took the shame for us, ignoring, or despising it as something that He was happy to do for us. Being hung naked as a criminal in front of a crowd of mockers will bring shame, shame of many varieties, even the variety that has been put on you.

Hebrews 12:2 says, "looking unto Jesus, the author and finisher of our faith, who for the joy that was set before Him endured the cross, despising the shame, and has sat down at the right hand of the throne of God."

One of Jesus' primary missions, as recorded in His mission statement of Isaiah 61, was the removal of shame. "Instead of your shame you shall have double honor, And instead of confusion they shall rejoice in their portion. Therefore in their land they shall possess double; Everlasting joy shall be theirs" (Isaiah 61:7).

If it is shame, then appropriate the blood of Jesus and its cleansing power to wash you as white as snow.

## It is all about our identity.
*If you really know who you are as God sees you, shame will loose its grip.*

Take a deep breath now and see who you really are through the eyes of Truth. The Word of God is the only true genealogy of who you are. If you know who you are, you will not behave like who you are not. Truth is the most powerful weapon in the universe.

*Jesus bore our shame on the Cross and gave us His clean identity.*

"I gave My back to those who struck Me, And My cheeks to those who plucked out the beard; I did not hide My face from shame and spitting" (Isaiah 50:6).

The Word of God is the only thing that can renew our mind to the Truth! Study and meditate on these truths, confess the Scriptures, determine to believe them no matter what your senses tell you, until they renew your mind.

However, you will never achieve a renewed mind with the truth of God's Word until you truly give God the truth about yourself. You must open up all the "compartments" in your soul. You do this by simply talking to God like a best friend. Tell Him all of your feelings, sins, anxieties, unforgiveness, and all of your low self-esteem. Hide nothing! He cannot show you who you are in Him, until you show Him who you are without Him. Failure to do this will keep you in bondage!

***We are supposed to obtain our true identity from God through His Word.***

I urge you to study the story in Numbers chapters 13 and 14 about the Israelites and the twelve spies in the Promised Land. God had promised them the Promised Land. Only two of the twelve spies, Joshua and Caleb, had enough faith in God's Word to see themselves as victorious over their enemies. The other ten said, "There we saw the giants (the descendants of Anak came from the giants); and we were like grasshoppers in our own sight, and so we were in their sight" (Numbers 13:33).

***Satan sows seeds to produce a wrong self-image in us.***

In Matthew 13:1-23 Jesus told His disciples a parable about the Word of God being planted in their hearts as a seed. He explained how it worked and how Satan tried to keep it from working. Then He explained that not only would Satan try to steal the Word out of their hearts, but that he (Satan) also was a seed sower.

"Another parable He put forth to them, saying: 'The kingdom of heaven is like a man who sowed good seed in his field; but while men slept, his enemy came and sowed tares among the wheat and went his way'" (Matthew 13:24-25).

**Following are some facts in the Word that you should meditate on.**

These facts are good seed, which will bear good fruit in your life.

***1. You were hopelessly lost.***

That means that someone else had to search for you. Ephesians 2:12 (a & b) says, "that at that time you were without Christ,...having no hope and without God in the world."

***2. You were dead in your sins.***

There is no way out for a dead man, except to receive life. Ephesians 2:1 says, "And you He made alive, who were dead in trespasses and sins."

The blood Jesus shed on the Cross did more than remove and forgive your sins. Notice in these Scriptures that we only have forgiveness and redemption "IN HIM." Colossians 1:14 says, "in whom we have redemption through His blood, the forgiveness of sins." Ephesians 1:7 says, "In Him we have redemption through His blood, the forgiveness of sins, according to the riches of His grace."

**3. *Our original "forgiveness" is often misunderstood.***

Many feel that they are the same person but now Jesus has just removed, "excused," or forgiven their sins.

*Wrong! You were crucified with Christ.*

The first thing God did for you was to "put you" in Christ to experience a co-death with Him. Your old Adamic nature, the "first you," had no hope of being cleaned up. You had to die. The wages of sin is death. The Good News is that you did die. You were already "in Christ" when He was crucified; you just needed to discover it and believe and accept it.

**4. *You were already "In Christ" when the following events took place.***

"I have been crucified with Christ; it is no longer I who live, but Christ lives in me; and the life which I now live in the flesh I live by faith in the Son of God, who loved me and gave Himself for me" (Galatians 2:20).

**5. *You died with Christ.***

"For if we have been united together in the likeness of His death, certainly we also shall be in the likeness of His resurrection" (Romans 6:5).

**6. *You were buried with Christ.***

" Therefore we were buried with Him through baptism into death" (Romans 6:4a). "...Having been buried with Him in baptism, in which you also were raised with Him through faith in the working of God, who raised Him from the dead" (Colossians 2:12a, NASB). If you are having a difficult time with identity, I suggest memorizing Romans chapter 6. Doing that had a profound affect on my life.

**7. *You were made alive with Christ.***

Colossians 2:13 says "And you, being dead in your trespasses and the uncircumcision of your flesh, He has made alive together with Him, having forgiven you all trespasses." Ephesians 2:5 says, "even when we were dead in trespasses, made us alive together with Christ (by grace you have been saved)."

***8. You were raised with Christ. You are seated with Christ.***

Ephesians 2:5-6 (NIV) says, "[He God] made us alive with Christ even when we were dead in transgressions--it is by grace you have been saved. And God raised us up with Christ and seated us with him in the heavenly realms in Christ Jesuseven when we were dead in trespasses, made us alive together with Christ (by grace you have been saved), and raised us up together, and made us sit together in the heavenly places in Christ Jesus."

That is our legal standing with God today and the foundation of our legal rights. As far as the spiritual world is concerned, your position is with Christ in the heavenlies. You are in a seat of authority. Satan and your mind will tell you that you are not seated with Christ in the heavenlies, but that is a lie! You need to know that God seated you with Him while you were yet a sinner!

***9. You are a new creation.***

2 Corinthians 5:17 says, "Therefore, if anyone is in Christ, he is a new creation; old things have passed away; behold, all things have become new."

***You might ask, "How can this be?"***

Good question. God put us in Christ. 1 Corinthians 1:30 says, "But of Him you are in Christ Jesus, who became for us wisdom from God--and righteousness and sanctification and redemption." Being in Christ is like you were in your father and mother as a sperm and an egg. You inherited their history in your genealogy. Just imagine that you are a marker inside of a book. When the book is moved, the marker goes with it. When the book is put on the shelf, the marker goes on the shelf. If the book is burned, the marker is burned. If, by some miracle, the book is restored and put back on the shelf, so is the marker.

Your history, and who you in Christ, is the result of the Blood Covenant with God through Jesus' death on the Cross and His

## Chapter 12 – Shame – Guilt – It's all about your identity

resurrection.

### *10. You are righteous.*

Righteous means to have a right standing with God. A son (or daughter) is righteous with his father by birth. He is in the family and he has a right standing that the neighbor does not have. We are righteous by our new birth, not by anything we have done. 2 Corinthians 5:21 says, "For He made Him who knew no sin to be sin for us, that we might become the righteousness of God in Him." We are righteous because God put His life in us, not because of the way we act or live.

### *11. Satan's dominion over you is broken.*

Satan had dominion of your old nature, but your new nature is Christ's own Spirit that has already defeated Satan. Romans 6:8-10 says, "Now if we died with Christ, we believe that we shall also live with Him, knowing that Christ, having been raised from the dead, dies no more. Death no longer has dominion over Him. For the death that He died, He died to sin once for all; but the life that He lives, He lives to God." If the spirit of the world has had you living in fear, God will set you free right now!

Because of who you are in Christ, "bad things" no longer have power over you. Instead, you have power over them to convert them into blessings. Colossians 1:20 says, "and by Him to reconcile all things to Himself, by Him, whether things on earth or things in heaven, having made peace through the blood of His cross."

### *Why do I not feel the way these Scriptures say?*

I am very glad you asked. That is an important question. It took years for you to get the world's and the "other god's" view of yourself. You were trained with a guilt, sin, fear and curse consciousness, and it will take some time to get your mind renewed to the truth. From Satan's point of view, he is trying to steal the seed of the Word out of your heart. If he puts enough pressure on you with circumstances and guilt, you may stop believing.

## How do we accept this gift?

### 1. Make Jesus and His Word your Master, or Lord.

You must determine to believe the Word instead of your feelings and your old flesh patterns. You must determine to obey the Word. Obedience is integral part of believing. Romans 10:9-10 says, "that if you confess with your mouth the Lord Jesus and believe in your heart that God has raised Him from the dead, you will be saved. For with the heart one believes unto righteousness, and with the mouth confession is made unto salvation."

### 2. Be honest with God about your condition.

All things will be cleansed in the light, all things will be kept under bondage in the dark. You must bring your condition to the light, to Jesus in honesty. If you can agree with another person that can be powerful. However, use great caution with your confidence in others!

### 3. Forgive others and receive your own forgiveness.

### 4. Accept yourself for who you are and who God created you to be.

Know that God made you his "workmanship" which is also translated "poiema," or his original one-of-a-kind poem, Ephesians 2:10.

## How we treat others is a major issue.

Proverbs 14:35 says, "The king's favor *is* toward a wise servant, But his wrath *is against* him who causes shame."

We all need to be careful that we treat others in a way that the Lord would want us to treat them. We need to treat others with justification and not with condemnation and guilt. If we use guilt, shame and condemnation on people, even with good intentions, we are doing the work of the enemy and perhaps helping to cut of the life of God to the people we are trying to help. There may be times that the Lord would use us to help "lovingly convict" certain people for their good. I have experienced that, but one should be extremely careful to know for sure that it is the Lord who is leading this effort, lest we fall into horrible error and inflict terrible injury on another.

## Chapter 12 – Shame – Guilt – It's all about your identity

**Cannery Row.**
In John Steinbeck's book Cannery Row there is a great study about guilt and shame. Doc, as a young baseball player, had thrown a pitch, which inflicted permanent brain damage on the batter (I forget his name, but we will call him Joe). Joe wandered the beach as a bum the rest of his life. Motivated by guilt, Doc would go out to find him to feed him and care for him. Doc was building a marine museum and almost had it finished. Once when Doc was out of town, a drunk used the place for a drunken party, broke up all his aquariums and destroyed Doc's dream. When Doc discovered that this drunk had done the damage, he immediately forgave him, knowing that putting guilt and/or shame on another being was too terribly painful, even more painful than losing his life's dream. It was amazing to see the sensitivity of not wanting to paste guilt and/or shame on another. If you have ever been delivered from guilt or shame by Jesus, you will be very sensitive to protect others from its horrible effects.

**Prayer.**
Shame leads to self-hatred. Where there is self-hatred we must first confess and repent.

"Lord, I confess the sin of self-hatred. I repent for any self-hatred I've carried in my body, soul or spirit. Please forgive me and wash me clean of all self-hatred. I bring all the old ways of thinking, believing, feeling and acting to the Cross and ask You to bring that old man to death with all its shame. Resurrect Your likeness in its place. Give me Your ways of thinking, believing, feeling and acting. Renew my mind and transform my soul."

"Jesus, You are my Lord. I confess to you my guilt and shame. I bring to you what others have done to me, what I have done to others, and those deeds that I did that were sin before you. Thank You, Lord, for Your blood that was shed so that all of these deeds could be forgiven and removed. Thank You, Lord, for bearing my shame and guilt even though You did not deserve it. Thank You for being called guilty and for being shamed and abused while You were totally innocent and I was totally guilty.

Now I simply believe Your Word which says that I am not condemned and that my conscience is cleansed."

"Who may ascend into the hill of the LORD? Or who may stand in His holy place? He who has clean hands and a pure heart, Who has not lifted up his soul to an idol, Nor sworn deceitfully" (Psalm 24:3-4).

## Chapter 13
## The War For Your Thought Life.
A step towards healing

Romans 12:1-2 says, "I beseech you therefore, brethren, by the mercies of God, that you present your bodies a living sacrifice, holy, acceptable to God, *which is* your reasonable service. And do not be conformed to this world, but be transformed by the renewing of your mind, that you may prove what *is* that good and acceptable and perfect will of God."

The Amplified Bible reads, "in view of [all] the mercies of God." I believe that this refers to the mercies of God that Paul has written about in Romans chapters 1-8. Chapters 9, 10 and 11 are parenthetical, and Paul's thought process continues again in chapter 12. Paul is saying that when you look back and realize all of God's mercies towards you that your reasonable response would certainly be to offer your body a living sacrifice, especially your mind. In other words, that is the least you can do. In the Amplified version, it is called, "your reasonable (rational, intelligent) service and spiritual worship." Notice also, that the promise for having your mind transformed is that you would realize, or prove, the perfect will of God.

That word *prove* in Romans 12:2 is the same word used in the refining of gold or silver, therefore we know that this process will include pain. Do you want the perfect will of God for your life? Offer your mind, your thinking, to the process of transformation!

The word *transformed* is interesting. The Strong's Concordance defines it as:

*Metamorphoo: transfigure, transform, change. To change into another form, to transform, to transfigure.* Christ's appearance was changed and was resplendent with divine brightness on the mount of transfiguration.

### We need a total change in our thinking.
Even after we become born-again children of God, our old thinking needs to change to see who God has made us to be. He

## Chapter 13 – The War For Your Thought Life

does not want us insecure and inferior. He wants us to know that we are New Creations in Christ, part of a new race of people. Christ now lives within us and has caused us to be re-born into a new race with dominion over Satan. We have returned to the original pattern God intended for man. However, now we have the resurrected Spirit of Christ, something Adam and Eve did not enjoy.

*Why do we need a change in our thinking?*

We need a change in our thinking from the lie to the truth. Truth is the most powerful weapon in the world. It is so valuable that it is guarded by a bodyguard of lies.

*What we think will affect our speech, and what we speak will affect our lives.*

Luke 6:45 says, "A good man out of the good treasure of his heart brings forth good; and an evil man out of the evil treasure of his heart brings forth evil. For out of the abundance of the heart his mouth speaks."

James 3:4-6 says, "Look also at ships: although they are so large and are driven by fierce winds, they are turned by a very small rudder wherever the pilot desires. Even so the tongue is a little member and boasts great things. See how great a forest a little fire kindles! And the tongue *is* a fire, a world of iniquity. The tongue is so set among our members that it defiles the whole body, and sets on fire the course of nature; and it is set on fire by hell."

## Our weapons are for protecting our thought life and our covenant rights of our "knowing" Him.

2 Corinthians 10:3-5 (KJV) says, "For though we walk in the flesh, we do not war after the flesh: (For the weapons of our warfare *are* not carnal, but mighty through God to the pulling down of strong holds;) Casting down imaginations, and every high thing that exalteth itself against the *knowledge* of God, and bringing into captivity every thought to the obedience of Christ."

Your thinking process is able to control the rest of your life. That is why this Scripture talks about the violent spiritual warfare against the biggest possible hindrance in our walk with God, that being, "stinking thinking."

*There is a war for our thought life.*

God made us Kings and Priests. Kings make war and priests represent man to God and God to man, or in other words, ministry. We cannot have wholeness in our lives nor ministry to others without engaging in the warfare aimed at our minds and thought life.

**Knowing God is everything.**
*The Blood Covenant is about knowing Him.*

Knowing is a word that suggests the most intimate personal contact, more than intellectual knowledge. It is a close personal knowing. However, we are in a war for that. The war is in and for our minds. Our greatest task is to take our thoughts captive with the weapons God has given us. Jesus has already defeated Satan at the Cross. He has already given us a complete blood covenant. Our war is not to defeat Satan, but simply to defend what our rightful inheritance is. Furthermore, Jesus is the mediator of the blood covenant. He is there to make sure that we receive the blood covenant privileges. But remember, His name is The Word.

When you are "knowing" Jesus, present tense, you see Him alive here on earth, and the devil's plans are thwarted. However, if the devil can get control of your thoughts you will not know Jesus, and the devil's plans can succeed. Remember Jesus said to some in Matthew 7:23, "I never knew you."

*The removal of sin is what allows us to know Him. Jeremiah prophesied it.*

Jeremiah 24:7 and 31:34 says, "'Then I will give them a heart to know Me, that I *am* the LORD; and they shall be My people, and I will be their God, for they shall return to Me with their whole heart." "No more shall every man teach his neighbor, and every man his brother, saying, 'Know the LORD,' for they all shall know Me, from the least of them to the greatest of them, says the LORD. For I will forgive their iniquity, and their sin I will remember no more."

## Chapter 13 – The War For Your Thought Life

*If you are disconnected you live as a mere Gentile in the futility of your mind. If you do, you can nullify everything He wants to give you in and through His intimacy.* Sinful thinking can keep us from knowing Him. Ephesians 4:17 says, "This I say, therefore, and testify in the Lord, that you should no longer walk as the rest of the Gentiles walk, in the futility of their mind." Ephesians 4:23 says, "and be renewed in the spirit of your mind."

**Paul prayed that the church would know and experience God.**

**Ephesians 3:16-20 (Amplified Bible) says,**

*16 May He grant you out of the rich treasury of His glory to be strengthened and reinforced with mighty power in the inner man by the [Holy] Spirit [Himself indwelling your innermost being and personality].*

*17 May Christ through your faith [actually] dwell (settle down, abide, make His permanent home) in your hearts! May you be rooted deep in love and founded securely on love,*

*18 That you may have the power and be strong to apprehend and grasp with all the saints [God's devoted people, the experience of that love] what is the breadth and length and height and depth [of it];*

*19 [That you may really come] to know [practically, through experience for yourselves] the love of Christ, which far surpasses mere knowledge [without experience]; that you may be filled [through all your being] unto all the fullness of God [may have the richest measure of the divine Presence, and become a body wholly filled and flooded with God Himself]!*

*20 Now to Him Who, by (in consequence of) the [action of His] power that is at work within us, is able to [carry out His purpose and] do superabundantly, far over and above all that we [dare] ask or think [infinitely beyond our highest prayers, desires, thoughts, hopes, or dreams].*

## Chapter 13 – The War For Your Thought Life

Disciplining our thinking is a major task. Being lazy in the things of God in this life can affect us eternally.

Please know that we are not attempting to minimize the mercy and grace of God, the finished work of Jesus at the Cross, by suggesting some sort of salvation by works program or legalism. We are not suggesting that God is sitting back to watch how well we perform. No! He did it all. However, He also warned us that we would have to overcome, which is a term used in warfare. Our new birth is free. However, our staying plugged into the life of God, maintaining a real time intimacy with Him, allows Him to make us whole, to use us for His glory, and to bring His Kingdom purposes to this earth.

Spiritual warfare and discipline is needed to keep our thought life plugged into His Word and to resist Satan's thought bombs. Satan's task is to take over our thoughts so that he can unplug us from God's life. Our mind is Satan's best and most fruitful battlefield.

**God already provided the solution.**
*We just need to conform our thinking to His truth.*

You need to know for sure, that God Himself did everything needed to completely heal your wounds through Jesus' work. His life, death, resurrection and ascension accomplished more than enough to completely make you whole. Our part is to believe the truth. Renewing our mind to truth is a process that can take time. It is real even when it does not seem real. Our minds really can and do change. That change affects our entire life. I can testify to this truth in my own life and in the lives of multitudes of others.

My contributing-editor Michael Vincent tells how he overcame the strongholds of feeling stupid, inadequate, and not good enough. When Michael started school they told him from the first day that he would not learn like the other children. Everyday he went to school and the lie was being reinforced stronger and stronger, the fortress was being built. Year after year Michael fell further behind his peers in school. Due to his belief system he gave up trying to learn. At age 37, after 20 years of drug and alcohol addiction Michael found himself in a Christian-based drug and alcohol program. Once in the program he had to start memorizing scripture. At first, his "right to be right" and his rebellious heart wanted to hold on to the lie that he could not do it. After help, encouragement and prayer from the other men in the program he started memorizing scripture one at a time. It was not long before he had memorized all sixteen passages to stay in the program. One day in prayer he felt overwhelmed with the anger and resentment he had towards God because he always believed that God had made a mistake when he created him. After asking and receiving forgiveness from God he renounced the vow that he would never be able to learn. Then he thanked God for creating him believing that God did not make a mistake and he came to a place that even if he never read a book that he was just who God created him to be. At this moment there was a spiritual bondage broken off his life. God stilled his soul, gave him patience to read one word at a time and to start memorizing more scripture. Today, many years later, he has read hundreds of Christian books; he reads the Bible every day and is walking victoriously over the stronghold that existed for most of his life.

***The real truth is radical.***

For instance, Galatians 2:20 says, "I have been crucified with Christ; it is no longer I who live, but Christ lives in me; and the *life* which I now live in the flesh I live by faith in the Son of God, who loved me and gave Himself for me."

Romans 6:3-4 says, "Or do you not know that as many of us as were baptized into Christ Jesus were baptized into His death? Therefore we were buried with Him through baptism into death, that just as Christ was raised from the dead by the glory of the Father, even so we also should walk in newness of life."

Not only was your sin taken away, but also the person who sinned was put to death, and you were raised with Christ and are now seated with Him in heavenly places. You were actually born-again into an entire new race of people. When you begin to believe this truth, then your mind will be renewed. When that happens the process of inner healing can have its full freedom to

## Chapter 13 – The War For Your Thought Life

do its work in you. This is a lot deeper work than emotional healing. Even non-believers can receive emotional healing. However, only a child of God who is a disciple can be supernaturally transformed!

When your mind is renewed to really believe, not just mentally, but by revelation knowledge, that you really have been crucified with Christ, that you were really in Him when He was nailed to the Cross, then you will experience real freedom.

### Examples of damaging thoughts.
We can receive thoughts:
1. Against the true character of God,
2. Against our true identity in Christ.
3. Against others.

Loving God with all of our mind is a command. "Jesus said to him, 'You shall love the LORD your God with all your heart, with all your soul, and with all your mind. This is *the* first and great commandment. And *the* second *is* like it: You shall love your neighbor as yourself'" (Matthew 22:37-39).

### Where do inordinate thoughts come from?
So many thoughts come involuntarily from past broken relationships, especially from our fathers. Our past or present negative circumstances can give us negative thoughts. Damaging thoughts can also come from our present friends, or from what we focus our eyes and ears upon, and what we determine to set our minds upon. Satan's army can shoot direct thoughts at your mind.

When Jesus saves us, our spirits are made whole. When we go to Heaven our bodies are made new and whole. However, while here, on earth, we are to pursue the healing and prosperity of our souls, which include our will, mind and emotions. Romans 12:1-2 makes it clear that we are to pursue the renewing of our minds.

While we are born again to a new species of beings, we experience traces of the "flesh," the "old man" in our thought life.

## Chapter 13 – The War For Your Thought Life

We are not of two identities as some try to teach, there are not two people living inside us. We are a new resurrected being, a new creation in Christ. However, the "old man" has left old thoughts in our minds, and that is where the battle rages. God wants it renewed, Satan wants it to control us.

**Take your thoughts captive.**
*When you hear a word, a seed is planted; that is a fact of life!*
Words become thoughts then they bear fruit. Satan also plants words, which become thoughts (Matthew 13:25). These thoughts eventually bear Satan's fruit.

*Here is a rather simple system for taking your thoughts captive and renewing your mind.*

*1. Take your thoughts captive.* Airports now have security checkpoints that screen each person and each piece of luggage for dangerous items before boarding an airplane. You do the same thing. When you sense a thought, stop, and ask, "Does this thought carry dangerous consequences? Is this thought profitable for me to live a godly life? Is this thought from Satan, or my flesh?" At that point, you simply make a decision to say to that thought, "I do not allow you entrance. I take you captive and evict you in the name of Jesus."

After some practice you will better recognize those thoughts that come from God. Often God's thoughts come as spontaneous thoughts. Sometimes to me they feel like a bolt of lighting that just zooms through your spirit.

*Replace your thoughts with godly thoughts.* You cannot just leave a vacuum; you must fill your mind with something good.

*2. Begin to meditate on the Word of God.* Ask God to help you find a Scripture, then write it down and memorize it. "Chew" on it and meditate upon it all day long. Think of a Bible story and imagine it in your mind. Images are how we think. That is why in our key Scripture, 2 Corinthians 10:3-5 quoted above, it says to cast down imaginations, or in some translations, the word arguments is used. The word is more akin to imaginations. Our mind works in pictures, or imaginations, rather than in words.

***3. Speak the Word.*** Make a habit of speaking the Word of God out loud. You cannot think bad thoughts and speak something different. Try it.

**Summary.**
In summary, Jesus gave us the Blood Covenant that removes our sin. One of the main benefits of that is that we may know Him in an intimate way. When we are in the present tense of knowing Him, His power works in us, for us and for others in the world. Satan knows that our thought life can keep us from the power of God; therefore that is where he concentrates his "big guns."

**"I took My thoughts captive for you. Will you do the same for Me?"**
Philippians 2:5 says, "Let this mind be in you which was also in Christ Jesus..." The verses following state that His "mind" is, humility and the desire to take up His Cross. We must take up our cross when we sense an inordinate thought trying to control us.

**The following is a quote from Purpose Driven Life Daily Devotions.**
PurposeDrivenLife.com is a Ministry of Saddleback Church, 1 Saddleback Pkwy, Lake Forest, CA 92630. Tel: (800) 633-8876.

*Be careful how you think; your life is shaped by your thoughts. Proverbs 4:23 (GNT)*

*One of the great psychological discoveries of the past century is that your thoughts control your actions. If you want to change the way you act, you must first change how you think.*

*Actually, thousands of years ago, Solomon pointed this out when he wrote, "Be careful how you think; your life is shaped by your thoughts" (Proverbs 4:23 GNT).*

*The Bible says our thoughts influence six areas of our lives:*

*My interpretation influences my situation. It's not what happens to me that matters as much as how I choose to see*

## Chapter 13 – The War For Your Thought Life

*it. The way I react will determine whether the circumstance makes me better or bitter. I can view everything as an obstacle or an opportunity for growth – a stumbling block or a stepping stone. "Consider it pure joy, my brothers, whenever you face trials of many kinds, because you know that the testing of your faith develops perseverance. Perseverance must finish its work so that you may be mature and complete, not lacking anything" (James 1:2-4 NIV).*

*My impressions influence my depressions. In other words, my mind affects my mood; my thinking determines my feelings. If I'm feeling depressed, it's because I'm choosing to think depressing thoughts – about my work, family, or anything else. While you cannot always control a feeling, you* can *choose what you think about, which will control how you feel." Hear me and answer me. My thoughts trouble me and I am distraught . . ." (Psalm 55:2 NIV).*

*My beliefs influence my behavior. We always act according to our beliefs, even when those ideas are false. For instance, as a child, if you believed a shadow in your bedroom at night was a monster, your body reacted in fear (adrenaline and jitters) even though it wasn't true. That's why it's so important to make sure you are operating on true information! Your convictions about yourself, about life, and about God influence your conduct. "If you hold to my teaching, you are really my disciples" (John 8:31 NIV).*

*My self-talk influences my self-esteem. You are constantly talking to yourself unconsciously. When you walk into a room full of strangers, what do you tend to think about yourself? To develop more confidence you're going to have to stop running yourself down! "As he thinks in his heart, so is he" (Proverbs 23:7 NKJV).*

*My attitude influences my ability. Winners expect to win. Your perception controls your performance. Mohammed Ali only lost two fights in his career. Before both of them, he said something that he hadn't said before other fights: "If I should lose this fight [...]." "All things are possible to him who believes" (Mark 9:23 NKJV).*

*My imagination influences my aspirations. In other words, your dreams determine your destiny. To accomplish anything, you must first have a mission, a goal, a hope, a vision. "Where there is no vision, the people perish" (Proverbs 29:18 KJV).*

The tearing down of these strongholds could take years depending on how deep the wound and how long you have been believing this stronghold. We can testify in our own lives that by taking thoughts captive immediately, by meditating on the Word, memorizing scripture, taking our daily moral inventory and journaling to God, these fortresses will be destroyed quicker. The more you pursue God, trust in Him, and allow His love to help you see the truth, the more you will overcome. Where the Spirit of the Lord is there is freedom.

## Chapter 14
## Living Like Who You Really Are
You can't be free if you don't live like who you really are.

In this book we have provided an opportunity through each chapter to realize God's inner healing provisions. We emphasized the power of His Cross for your healing needs and the transformation of your life. Now in this chapter we want to point out some of your responsibilities.

In our previous chapters we emphasized knowing who you are in Christ by faith in the Word of God. We stated that really getting an inner revelation on this will begin to transform your outer life. We also emphasized that you must be totally transparent with God in order to have that kind of faith to see and believe that you were really crucified with Christ and have been resurrected with Him already. We also emphasized that your thinking must be changed, your mind must be renewed to really see this amazing revelation.

However, we can neutralize God's mighty power if we do not practice "Walking in the Spirit," or in other words, making a determination to live a life of love. Galatians 5:6 says, "For in Christ Jesus neither circumcision nor uncircumcision avails anything, but faith working through love."

**Be careful of extremes.**

Like many spiritual issues, walking in the Spirit can be misunderstood from two different extremes, both of which will cause great failure in our lives.

One extreme is living your life as if anything goes. Some people think that God's love and God's grace excuses them from making an effort to be overcomers and to allow Christ to be formed in them. They mistake this as grace.

The other extreme is living your life in a "perfect or nothing" attitude. These people realize that God wants them to change, but when they make mistakes, sin, and fail to change, they become condemned, feel overwhelmed, and give up.

## Chapter 14 – Living Like Who You Really Are

***The truth is stated in Romans chapter 8.***

In Romans 6 Paul wrote about the wonderful finished work of Christ. In Romans 7 Paul then went on to say that he could not live his life as if Christ's work was finished. Then, in Romans 8 he gives the solution.

**Romans 8:1-6 says,**

*1* There is *therefore now no condemnation to those who are in Christ Jesus, who do not walk according to the flesh, but according to the Spirit.*

*2 For the law of the Spirit of life in Christ Jesus has made me free from the law of sin and death.*

*3 For what the law could not do in that it was weak through the flesh, God* did *by sending His own Son in the likeness of sinful flesh, on account of sin: He condemned sin in the flesh,*

*4 that the righteous requirement of the law might be fulfilled in us who do not walk according to the flesh but according to the Spirit.*

*5 For those who live according to the flesh set their minds on the things of the flesh, but those* who live *according to the Spirit, the things of the Spirit.*

*6 For to be carnally minded* is *death, but to be spiritually minded* is *life and peace.*

Notice that he said, "walk" according to flesh or the Spirit. Walk is an ongoing active verb. It means continuing to live in one manner or the other. It does not say that if you make a mistake you will be condemned. Paul is not talking about perfectionism, but rather about never giving up. You will see in the definition of walking in the Spirit below, that we will make mistakes. However, my belief is that God sees our trying, He sees our heart of attempting to please Him, and most of all He sees our repentance when we fail, and He says, "Come on now, get up, I am proud of you, you can make it."

## Chapter 14 – Living Like Who You Really Are

**When the pain of what you are in exceeds the pain of change, then you can be healed.**

That is an expression I often hear from Michael and Karen Vincent, my friends and co-editors. Now that we know who God is, we know that Jesus paid the price for our inner healing, and we know who Jesus made us to be in Him, we need to make lifestyle changes to conform to who we really are. It is not enough that God has done all these wonderful things for us if we do not make daily, even hourly, choices that will conform our lifestyle to match our true identity.

One major change you must make is to determine to fellowship with God in His Word. I am not referring about simply praying for your needs. Rather I am suggesting that you must take time to soak in the Word, pour out your heart to Him, practice a daily time of praise and thanksgiving, and in some way record your time with Him, preferably in writing, which we call journaling. Faith only comes by hearing the Word. When you hear the Word, revelation has an opportunity to come into your heart. When that happens His light does miracles within and for you.

**Warning!**

Many believers do not take their prayer life, their time of communing with God, seriously. I can usually detect those people who are attempting to walk in the Spirit. They seem to just have a "scent" about them. I am not referring to immature believer, or young believers, or those who are not educated in the Word of God, quite often they can have a closer communion with God than older believers. Taking time to cleanse your heart and to commune with God is what brings life, and it is what makes life worth living. It is what will provide for all of your needs. It is what gives Jesus joy.

*Christ needs to be formed in you.*

When you need the Holy Spirit more than life itself, then Christ will be formed in you. Galatians 4:19 says, "My little children, for whom I labor in birth again until Christ is formed in you." Oswald Chambers wrote, "The teaching is not Christ for me unless I am determined to have Christ formed in me."

## Chapter 14 – Living Like Who You Really Are

***We are saved by faith.***

Romans 4:2-6 says, "For if Abraham was justified by works, he has *something* to boast about, but not before God. For what does the Scripture say? "Abraham believed God, and it was accounted to him for righteousness." Now to him who works, the wages are not counted as grace but as debt. But to him who does not work but believes on Him who justifies the ungodly, his faith is accounted for righteousness, just as David also describes the blessedness of the man to whom God imputes righteousness apart from works."

***Our faith is completed and endorsed by works.***

James 2:14 says, "What *does it* profit, my brethren, if someone says he has faith but does not have works? Can faith save him?"

James 2:17-18 says, "Thus also faith by itself, if it does not have works, is dead. But someone will say, "You have faith, and I have works." Show me your faith without your works, and I will show you my faith by my works."

***Obedience to the King is needed.***

John 14:21 says, "He who has My commandments and keeps them, it is he who loves Me. And he who loves Me will be loved by My Father, and I will love him and manifest Myself to him."

The Bible is clear that we are saved from hell both in eternity and while we live on earth when we make Jesus our Lord. Making Him Lord means to give up our independence and to obey Him as our King. Notice in the verse above that the more we obey Him, the more He makes Himself real to us. Then it becomes a continuous cycle; we obey, He manifests Himself, then we see Him more and obey Him more. Soon, we become one with Him and He is glorified through the fruit we bear.

**Beware of only seeking God for your own comfort.**

I have known people who have had some encounter with God, but then have assumed that since God is love, then He will be okay with us no matter how we live. He just sort of comforts us and does not want us to feel any obligations.

***Comfort only comes after the fear of the Lord.***

## Chapter 14 – Living Like Who You Really Are

Acts 9:31 says, "Then the churches throughout all Judea, Galilee, and Samaria had peace and were edified. And walking in the **fear [respect and reverential fear]** of the Lord and in the **comfort** of the Holy Spirit, they were multiplied."

*Our works are not really our works; they are the works of grace by Christ living His live in and through us.*

Philippians 2:12-13 says, "Therefore, my beloved, as you have always obeyed, not as in my presence only, but now much more in my absence, work out your own salvation with fear and trembling; for it is God who works in you both to will and to do for *His* good pleasure."

*Faith works through love.*

You can study the Word all day and all night, meditate upon it and confess it until you pass out, but if you are not walking in love it will be for naught.

*Tear down your idols.*

In Judges chapters 6-8 Gideon and the Israelites were in bondage even while living in the Promised Land. God came and had many dealings with Gideon preparing him to be a deliverer for Israel. God developed a close friendship with Gideon and showed him the blood covenant. Gideon began to change his thinking from being a poor old defeated worm to being a mighty warrior for God. However, Gideon had to take a stand and tear down the family idols. Like Gideon, you will not be able to stand against your enemies unless you walk in love and forsake your old ways.

**Walking in the Spirit.**

Galatians 5:16 says, "I say then: Walk in the Spirit, and you shall not fulfill the lust of the flesh." Ephesians 4:1 says, "I, therefore, the prisoner of the Lord, beseech you to walk worthy of the calling with which you were called."

Romans 8:1 says, "There is therefore now no condemnation to those who are in Christ Jesus, who do not walk according to the flesh, but according to the Spirit." If you read on to Romans 8:8 you will find that God is serious about having us walk according to

## Chapter 14 – Living Like Who You Really Are

the Spirit and not according to the flesh. He states that there is victory for one lifestyle and total defeat for the other lifestyle.

Galatians 6:7-8 says, "Do not be deceived, God is not mocked; for whatever a man sows, that he will also reap. For he who sows to his flesh will of the flesh reap corruption, but he who sows to the Spirit will of the Spirit reap everlasting life."

Walking in the Spirit is a simple, but a different way to live and the easiest way I know to be right with God on a daily basis. It is a process that goes like this:

1. You continue to look into the Word of God (mirror) and ask God to show you how to live. Ask Him, and seek out what His standards are for your life. For instance, it says to not lie, to treat your friends with love, to submit to your authorities, to treat your family with kindness, to not get drunk, to not be selfish, to not be angry, always forgive not matter what, etc.

2. You determine to live the way God wants you to, in love, knowing that only God in you can walk a life worthy of the Lord.

3. When you fail, and you will, be totally honest with yourself, God, and others around you. Repent (turn) quickly. The promise is that when we repent (turn) that the Kingdom of God is at hand, or within our reach.

4. Confess your sin to God. 1 John 1:9 says, "If we confess our sins, He is faithful and just to forgive us our sins and to cleanse us from all unrighteousness."

5. Confess what the Word of God says about your situation in a positive way, i.e., Galatians 2:20 that says, "I have been crucified with Christ; it is no longer I who live, but Christ lives in me; and the life which I now live in the flesh I live by faith in the Son of God, who loved me and gave Himself for me."

6. As you continue to live this way those old habits and old sinful ways begin to disappear. The grace of God takes over and gives you the character of God instead of your old character.

7. Grace kicks in for your sin. You did not get righteous by the things you did, so your righteousness is still there, it just has some dirt on it. While you walk in the Spirit, God gives you grace for your mistakes, and He takes the penalty of the sin, and gives

## Chapter 14 – Living Like Who You Really Are

you overcoming power to deal with any consequences of the sin committed, and in that, you receive a blessing that you do not deserve.

8. Not only does grace kick in for your sin, not only does God give you a blessing that you did not deserve, but the grace you receive is actually the power that gets rid of the sin (or the problem) you are dealing with in the first place. Look at Zechariah 4:7 (KJV) which says, "Who *art* thou, O great mountain? before Zerubbabel [a type of Jesus] *thou shalt become* a plain: and he shall bring forth the headstone *thereof with* shoutings, *crying*, Grace, grace unto it." God speaks "grace" to your situation, and the mountain is removed!

**Hang on; there is some Good News in this chapter!**
When you confess your sin to God, it goes onto Jesus on the Cross, and from there to the grave. Do you remember what happens after the grave? That's right, resurrection!

When you sow your sin it ends up in the grave and God resurrects it into something beautiful; the likeness of His character!

1 Corinthians 15:42 says, "So also is the resurrection of the dead. The body is sown in corruption, it is raised in incorruption."

Galatians 6:8, says, "For he who sows to his flesh will of the flesh reap corruption, but he who sows to the Spirit will of the Spirit reap everlasting life."

Paul stated that we could actually experience this resurrected power while still in this body. Philippians 3:10-11 (Amplified Bible) says, "[For my determined purpose is] that I may know Him [that I may progressively become more deeply and intimately acquainted with Him, perceiving and recognizing and understanding the wonders of His Person more strongly and more clearly], and that I may in that same way come to know the power outflowing from His resurrection [which it exerts over believers], and that I may so share His sufferings as to be continually transformed [in spirit into His likeness even] to His death, [in the hope] That if possible I may attain to the [spiritual and moral] resurrection [that lifts me] out from among the dead [even while in the body]."

***How does this work?***

It works in many different ways in our lives, including making it through sorrows, overcoming difficulties, suffering, and trials in our lives. However, here we want to show you how "Walking in the Spirit" utilizes God's resurrection power for your sin and sinful attitudes!

**Now here is a list that we use in our lesson The Flowing River as a guide for allowing God to uncover those attitudes and actions in us that do not line up with God's character.**

## A spiritual checkup

- **Love** - Are you treating others with the unconditional love of God?
- **Selfishness** - Putting your own needs over the needs of others. Love is concerned with the welfare of the other person; are you more concerned with yourself and how you feel?
- **Stealing** - Can you remember taking money for property that was not yours?
- **Cheating** - Did you get anything from anyone unfairly?
- **Lying** - Any designed form of deception.
- **Slander** - Speaking evil of someone. You do not have to lie to slander. Have you spoken about others without love?
- **Immorality** - Are you guilty of stirring up desires that you could not righteously feed? Sexual vice, all impurity, even against your own body.
- **Drunkenness**, drugs sorcery, carousing.
- **Foul or polluted language**, evil words, unwholesome or worthless talk. Filthiness, foolish, silly, and corrupt talk.
- **Envy** - Behind the talk of other's failures and faults usually lurks envy.
- **Ingratitude** - How many times have others done things for you that you are not grateful for?

## Chapter 14 – Living Like Who You Really Are

- **Judging** – Do you criticize others thinking that you really understand what is in their hearts? Maybe you don't really know their very depths and how God is dealing with them.
- **Anger** - Have you been bad-tempered?
- **Cursing** - Have you used gutter language?
- **Needless silly talk.** Talking and acting like a moron. Jests and practical jokes that tend to undermine the sacred and precious standards of life. Have you made fun of an ethnic group or a certain part of the world, a state or region in your country, or some politician? Ethnic and regional jokes have no place in holiness.
- **Hardness** - Did you fight back, murmur or return evil for evil?
- **Habits** - Have you continually over-indulged natural appetites; how about your eating habits?
- **Half-heartedness** - Can you remember times when you deliberately shirked your full share of responsibility?
- **Hindrance** - Have you destroyed another's confidence in you by needlessly taking up their time? Have you betrayed another's confidence in you?
- **Hypocrisy** - Did the life you lived before some people make all you said of Christ and His gospel a lie?
- **Broken Vows** - Is there a vow you made to God that you have not kept?
- **Unforgiveness** - Are you holding any resentment against anyone, friend or foe?
- **Divisions**, clicks, the party spirit of having differing groups.
- **Lustful,** rich and wasteful living, greediness. Overspending on shopping, wasting time.
- **Not treating** wives, husbands, children, and parents with love and honor.
- **Not being content**, being jealous of what others have and you do not have.
- **Love of money** - A person without any money can still have the love of money.
- **Idolatry** - Any desire in your life above your desire for God.

## Chapter 14 – Living Like Who You Really Are

- **Strife** - Have you stirred up strife by unneeded words?
- **Witchcraft** - Manipulating another to meet your needs.
- **Rebellion to authority** - Boss, teacher, parent, spiritual leader, etc.
- **Love of the World** - Includes: Sins of the eyes - What are you reading or watching? Lust of the flesh - What are you desiring? Pride of life - What part of your life do you think you can handle without God being involved? - Pretending in thought or life to be more or less than you really ARE.
- **Pride** is the greatest sin of all. Examine these areas:
- Do you focus on the failure of others or are you concerned with your own sense of spiritual need?
- Are you self-righteous and critical or compassionate and forgiving, looking for the best in others?
- Do you look down on others or esteem all others better than yourself?
- Are you independent and self-sufficient or dependent, recognizing your need for others?
- Must you maintain control or do you surrender control?
- Do you have to prove you are correct, or are you willing to yield the right to be correct?
- Do you have a demanding spirit or a giving spirit?
- Do you desire to be served or are you motivated to serve others?
- Do you desire to be promoted or are you happy when others are promoted?
- Do you need to receive the credit or are you happy when others are recognized?
- Do you feel confident in how much you know or are you humbled by how much you have yet to learn?
- Are you self-conscious or not concerned with yourself at all?
- Do you keep people at arm's length or do you risk getting close to others. Are you willing to take the risk of loving intimately?

## Chapter 14 – Living Like Who You Really Are

- Are you quick to blame others or do you accept responsibility?
- Are you unapproachable or easy to be entreated?
- Are you defensive when criticized or receive criticism with a humble and open heart?
- Are you concerned with being respected or being real?
- Are you concerned about what others think or what God thinks?
- Do you work to maintain your image or do you die to your reputation?
- Do you find it difficult to share your spiritual needs with others or are you willing to be open and transparent?
- Do you try to hide your sin or are you willing to be exposed when you are wrong?
- Do you have a hard time saying, "I was wrong, will you please forgive me?"
- When confessing sin, do you deal in generalities or do you deal in specifics?
- Are you remorseful over your sin when you get caught or are you grieved over your sin and quick to repent?
- When there is a misunderstanding or conflict, do you wait for others to come and ask forgiveness or do you take the initiative?
- Do you compare yourself with others and feel deserving of honor or do you compare yourself to the holiness of God and feel a desperate need for mercy?
- Do you think you have little or nothing to repent for or do you have a continual attitude of repentance?
- Do you think that everyone else needs revival or do you continually sense a need for a fresh encounter with the filling of the Holy Spirit?
- Are you proud when you are around a new Christian or do you delight in his/her zeal? Are you willing to learn from him/her?

## Chapter 14 – Living Like Who You Really Are

- Are you intimidated when you are around a more mature Christian, or are you hungry to learn from his/her experience?

**Now go ahead and sow some of the seeds of confession of sin and repent, then expect to reap the resurrected life of Jesus in return!**

**Another reference for a deeper spiritual check up is the Daily Moral Inventory by Dunkin.**

Here is the web link to view the Daily Moral Inventory chart.

http://www.isob-bible.org/freetobe2008/dailymoralnew.pdf

## Chapter 15 – Are You Still Struggling?

**Often we struggle with attempting to obey God. This chapter will encourage you as you see how the Apostle Paul broke through this issue. Not only did he break through, but the process he used increased his intimacy with God. It will do the same for you!**

### Matthew 7:21-29
*"21 "Not everyone who says to Me, 'Lord, Lord,' shall enter the kingdom of heaven, but he who does the will of My Father in heaven.*
*22 "Many will say to Me in that day, 'Lord, Lord, have we not prophesied in Your name, cast out demons in Your name, and done many wonders in Your name?'*
*23 "And then I will declare to them, 'I never knew you; depart from Me, you who practice lawlessness!'*
*24 "Therefore whoever hears these sayings of Mine, and does them, I will liken him to a wise man who built his house on the rock:*
*25 "and the rain descended, the floods came, and the winds blew and beat on that house; and it did not fall, for it was founded on the rock.*
*26 "But everyone who hears these sayings of Mine, and does not do them, will be like a foolish man who built his house on the sand:*
*27 "and the rain descended, the floods came, and the winds blew and beat on that house; and it fell. And great was its fall."*
*28 And so it was, when Jesus had ended these sayings, that the people were astonished at His teaching,*
*29 for He taught them as one having authority, and not as the scribes."*

## Chapter 15 – Are You Still Struggling?

**Paul's experience.**
**Romans 7:15-8:1**
*"15 For what I am doing, I do not understand. For what I will to do, that I do not practice; but what I hate, that I do.*
***16 If, then, I do what I will not to do, I agree with the law that it is good. [Look at verse 22 – The law is in him)***
*17 But now, it is no longer I who do it, but sin that dwells in me.*
*18 For I know that in me (that is, in my flesh) nothing good dwells; for to will is present with me, but how to perform what is good I do not find.*
*19 For the good that I will to do, I do not do; but the evil I will not to do, that I practice.*
*20 Now if I do what I will not to do, it is no longer I who do it, but sin that dwells in me.*
*21 I find then a law, that evil is present with me, the one who wills to do good.*
***22 For I endorse and delight in the Law of God in my inmost self [with my new nature]. (amp Bible)***

*23 But I see another law in my members, warring against the law of my mind, and bringing me into captivity to the law of sin which is in my members.*
***24 O wretched man that I am! Who will deliver me from this body of death?***
*25 I thank God--through Jesus Christ our Lord! So then, with the mind I myself serve the law of God, but with the flesh the law of sin.*
***8:1 There is therefore now no condemnation to those who are in Christ Jesus, who do not walk according to the flesh, but according to the Spirit."***

    To obey is very important, but we cannot obey unless we hear God speak. We can't hear Him speak without staying in good standing with Him, hour-by-hour, day-by-day. Take this example from the Apostle Paul. Notice, how he struggled with walking properly with the Lord and obeying Him, but he hated how he was

## Chapter 15 – Are You Still Struggling?

acting. Why? Notice in verse 16 above that Paul said that he agreed with the Law, that it was good. But what about us who are not as schooled in the law as Paul was? Okay, look at verse 22 in the Amplified Bible above. The Law of God lives in you now through the Holy Spirit. He will convict you of not obeying, or not living a life pleasing to the Lord. But you have to have a passion about this; you have to be so controlled by the Holy Spirit to such a degree that you can hear Him convict you. That way you will be able to live like Paul, sick and tired of your old self, but with the knowledge that God in you will cure the problem!

Read this Scripture above again and just imagine Paul, and now you, speaking to God with this honest pain. Speak to Him in this manner and He will connect with you in a new and living way.

Look at the amazing revelation that Paul received from the Lord after all this struggling. If we, like Paul in Romans 7-8, will "walk in the Spirit," God will continually cleanse us and give us amazing personal revelations.

*8:1 There is therefore now no condemnation to those who are in Christ Jesus, who do not walk according to the flesh, but according to the Spirit*

**Start to obey Him in little things first and then you will grow.**

## Chapter 16
## Spiritual Warfare
You can't be free if you don't know about Satan's tactics

**We need to know that we are actually living in a world within a world.**
The world that we can see is only a dim manifestation of the real invisible world that we can see with our spiritual eyes when the Lord opens them for us.

Within that real spiritual world there is God, demons, devils, and angels. There is the cosmos, or the world system, ruled by Satan. This is what is real. If we continually attempt to control and manipulate the tangible world, we are futile in our efforts. We must know that we are citizens of the spiritual world first.

Within that spiritual world we all start out as citizens of the "world system," Satan's kingdom. However, God gives us a choice to become citizens of Heaven and enter into the Kingdom of God.

Once we become citizens of the Kingdom of God, then we must:

*1. Know who we are* (Sit, Ephesians 2:6).

*2. Live like who we are* (Walk, Ephesians 4:1).

*3. And finally, know how to react to the spiritual enemy Satan* (Stand, Ephesians 6:11).

If we attempt to leave out any of the above three issues, we will not be living like Jesus intended for us to live.

The subject of spiritual war, the satanic kingdom and demons is vast, and we will by no means attempt to make this chapter all-inclusive. Rather we want to give an overview of some practical issues that all of us need to be aware of. There is a childlike simplicity that we wish to express.

**Following is a list a few of the most common ways that Satan operates and some of the very simple steps you can take to keep yourself safe from his wiles.**

*1. We live in a fallen world and we can experience "fallout."*

## Chapter 16 – Spiritual Warfare

"Stuff" just happens sometimes. You may not be the intended target of some satanic plot; you may just be experiencing sickness, disease, and other challenges and difficulties due to being subjected to a "fallen world" that has been subject to sin. However, neither do you need to be a victim to generational curses and other such things. When you experience "stuff" simply ask God to speak to you and show you how to pray, and if need be, what steps to take. When the pressure is on in this fashion, you will be really open to hearing God speak, and when He does, everything you are going through will be worth it.

God wants to take you through the seed bearing, fruit producing process. He will not leave you as an orphan in your trial if you truly seek Him with all your heart.

*2. If we don't "walk" like who we are, we will experience satanic influence.*

In our previous chapter we covered our "walk" with the Lord. We don't need to feel condemned when we are not perfect. However, God wants us to have a perfect and pure heart towards Him. If we come to Him for forgiveness, become obedient children, and ask Him to purify our heart, we can feel confident and rest in His care for us.

**3. Humility is the vital ingredient for spiritual warfare.**

Notice is Psalm 23 David said, "The Lord is my Shepherd." David saw himself as helpless and defenseless as the weakest and stupidest animal in the world, a sheep. Later in Psalm 23 David proclaimed victory over his enemies even in the valley of the shadow of death. Why? Because of his humility.

Job went through a breaking and finally **saw** God in a way he had never known Him before. That humbled Job. Then Satan lost his hold on Job and Job's friends.

There are many other Bible examples of humility being the main element in spiritual warfare. But Jesus is the best example.

**Jesus is called the Lamb of God.** Even Jesus saw Himself as a sheep while He was hear on earth under the care of His Father, His Shepherd. Jesus made no decisions without a long time in prayer with His Father. This humility is exactly why Jesus could defeat Satan at the Cross.

**Philippians 2:5-10.**
*"5 Let this mind be in you which was also in Christ Jesus,*
*6 who, being in the form of God, did not consider it robbery to be equal with God,*
*7 but made Himself of no reputation, taking the form of a bondservant, and coming in the likeness of men.*
*8 And being found in appearance as a man, He humbled Himself and became obedient to the point of death, even the death of the cross.*
*9 Therefore God also has highly exalted Him and given Him the name which is above every name,*
*10 that at the name of Jesus every knee should bow, of those in heaven, and of those on earth, and of those under the earth,"*

**4. Satan attempts to steal the Word of God after it is planted as a seed.**

This is a frontal attack to get you to not stand on the Word. You could also call this an attack for righteousness sake. God wants to provide for our needs through planting His Word in our heart and then watching it bear His fruit. This is what Satan's army fights against.

Satan was able to convince Adam and Eve that they could operate their lives without the Word of God (Genesis chapter 3). Satan tempted Jesus with the same issue in Luke chapter 4. He will use the same tactic on you. If Satan can get you to act out of your own independence without putting the Word of God first place in your life, he has succeeded. Satan wants you to act on your emotions and wrong thinking rather than on the Word.

Doubting the Word of God is Satan's main weapon. This is the essence of spiritual warfare. Without getting too complicated, spiritual warfare is primarily about believing or doubting God's Word. God wants us to trust His Word above all other evidence. Sometimes it is difficult to believe the truth we cannot see and feel with our five natural senses.

## Chapter 16 – Spiritual Warfare

Jesus was teaching His disciples in Mark chapter 4. Mark 4:9-11 says, "And He said to them, 'He who has ears to hear, let him hear!' But when He was alone, those around Him with the twelve asked Him about the parable. And He said to them, 'To you it has been given to know *the* mystery of the kingdom of God; but to those who are outside, all things come in parables.'"

**The entire Kingdom of God works like the parable in Mark chapter 4.**
Recently I received an email from a pastor in the Philippines who is studying our Grow or Die book, with the following comment. "Now I understand that God is a farmer and we are the Garden. I had no idea before but now I got it. Thanks so much." This is so simple yet profound. It is so deep, yet too many believers miss it just because it is so simple. Jesus called it the mystery of the Kingdom of God in Mark 4:11.

God plants the seeds of His Words in your heart (regardless of the condition of your heart). These seeds represent all of God's purposes for your life. Being born again is the first purpose. Next is being filled with the Spirit, being healed physically, emotionally, and mentally, and having your needs provided for by God. The Word brings you into your proper relationships in life, and provides all of God's further purposes for you, including ministry.

God uses His Word to impart His purposes to you. Fruit is how we are supposed to live our lives. Peter said that all we need for godliness and life is given to us by the promises of God, 2 Peter 1:3-4. His promises and the seed of His word are the same thing. Adam, before he sinned, was to bear fruit in the Garden. After he sinned, God told him that everything he need would be under a curse and he would have to obtain it by the sweat of his brow. Well, Jesus took the curse, and now we can return to normal and be fruit bearers.

I recently witnessed an entire missionary family radically changed by receiving revelation from our Grow or Die book. They discovered the seed/fruit process and were gloriously set free. The next time they went to preach a service, they didn't even preach,

## Chapter 16 – Spiritual Warfare

they just stood there and asked everyone to sing, and Jesus showed up. Dozens of people were at the altar getting delivered; twenty-five people were on the floor under the power of God. Jesus showed up because four people decided to be fruit bearers, and John 15:8 went into action!

***There is a childlike simplicity to how the Kingdom of God works.***

As we allow God to purify our hearts and we fellowship with Him, He speaks. As He speaks His Word to us, that Word becomes a seed in our hearts that is intended to bear fruit. The fruit is for our character, our needs and for our participation in glorifying Him to others. John 15:8 says, "By this My Father is glorified [made real and manifested to others], that you bear much fruit; so you will be My disciples." When you become a fruit bearer, wherever you go, Jesus will be made real to others. That, my friend, is powerful! No wonder Satan fights so hard to steal the Word, the seed, out of our hearts. No wonder Satan fights to hard to confuse people with all sorts of religious programs and theories just to keep the mystery of the Kingdom hidden.

***Notice in the Parable of the Sower that Satan comes to steal the Word.***

This is really the only weapon that Satan has against mankind, to steal the Word or to blind us from the Word. 2 Corinthians 4:4 says, "whose minds the god of this age has blinded, who do not believe, lest the light of the gospel of the glory of Christ, who is the image of God, should shine on them."

Once the Word is planted in your heart, you must "stand," or wait against adverse circumstances, until the plant matures. "Therefore take up the whole armor of God, that you may be able to withstand in the evil day, and having done all, to stand" (Ephesians 6:13).

Frontal attacks are countered by standing your position, keeping the territory you already have. You do that by continuing to refresh your identity in Christ, continually repenting your way through life as you "walk in the Spirit," and by verbally speaking the Word of God against the satanic beings that are in the attack.

## Chapter 16 – Spiritual Warfare

**I also believe that the Bible teaches us that during this waiting period, we are to use the Word of God as a sword.**
Ephesians 6:17b says, "the sword of the Spirit, which is the word of God."

This waiting period could be a matter of days, months, years, or decades. It matters not how long. During this time there are many purposes being accomplished, not the least of which is the purifying of our character. God may give us a promise, a vision; however, He must then purify us in order for us to be a vessel qualified to contain the vision.

*When we speak God's Word, Jesus takes it to the Father and asks Him to perform it.*

We are told in Hebrews 3:1 "Therefore, holy brethren, partakers of the heavenly calling, consider the Apostle and High Priest of our profession, Christ Jesus." Jesus takes our confession to the Father as our High Priest, and the Father sees to it that it is accomplished, provided it is the Word of God. The enemy also takes our confession, our negative confession, and accomplishes what we say.

When the Word of God is confessed and prayed over a person or a situation, it is powerful! Jesus created everything by His Word. Jesus *is* the Word. Jesus gave us the authority to use the Word as if it were He saying it!

John 1:1-3 says, "In the beginning was the Word, and the Word was with God, and the Word was God. He was in the beginning with God. All things were made through Him, and without Him nothing was made that was made."

John 16:23 says, "And in that day you will ask Me nothing. Most assuredly, I say to you, whatever you ask the Father in My name He will give you."

*Then we can enter into rest and let the Word do the work.*

Hebrews 4:1 says, "Therefore, since a promise remains of entering His rest, let us fear lest any of you seem to have come short of it."

Hebrews 4:12 says, "For the word of God is living and powerful, and sharper than any two-edged sword, piercing even to the division of soul and spirit, and of joints and marrow, and is a discerner of the thoughts and intents of the heart."

*Angels go to work when they hear God's Word.*

Psalm 103:20 says, "Bless the LORD, you His angels, who excel in strength, who do His word, heeding the voice of His word."

*Demons flee!*

Psalm 149:5-9 says, "Let the saints be joyful in glory; let them sing aloud on their beds. Let the high praises of God be in their mouth, and a two-edged sword in their hand, to execute vengeance on the nations, and punishments on the peoples (representing our spiritual enemies); to bind their kings with chains, and their nobles with fetters of iron; to execute on them the written judgment – this honor have all His saints. Praise the LORD!"

**The Passover.**

When the Passover was administered to Israel in Exodus 12, the Israelites were told to put the blood of an innocent lamb over their doors and the death angel (demon) would "pass over" and not hurt them. Jesus is the Lamb of God, and we can put His blood over our doors and over the doors of our loved ones and those that we pray for. How?

Revelation 12:11 says, "And they overcame him by the blood of the Lamb and by the word of their testimony, and they did not love their lives to the death."

The words of our mouth will apply the blood. Notice in Exodus 12 that as long as the lamb's blood stayed in the basin, it did no good. But when they took the hyssop, dipped it in the blood, and applied it to their door, then God and the devil could see it. The hyssop was a common weed that did not seem to have much value. The words of our mouth do not seem to have much value, but when we dip them into the Word of God (Who is Jesus Himself) and apply them as blood, God sees it and the devil sees it!

## Chapter 16 – Spiritual Warfare

**Be careful what you say!**

Mark 11:21-24 says "And Peter, remembering, said to Him, 'Rabbi, look! The fig tree which You cursed has withered away.' So Jesus answered and said to them, 'Have faith in God. For assuredly, I say to you, whoever says to this mountain, 'Be removed and be cast into the sea,' and does not doubt in his heart, but believes that those things he says will be done, he will have whatever he says. Therefore I say to you, whatever things you ask when you pray, believe that you receive *them*, and you will have *them*."

You may download a Word based prayer list at http://www.isob-bible.org/abf/prayerbook.htm

# Chapter 17
## Your Stone Is Rolled Away

Throughout this book we have been focusing on inner healing from the wounds of the past. These wounds of abuse, rejection, guilt, fear, poor self-esteem, unforgiveness, all become blockages to the abundant life that the Lord wants for us. For this chapter we will call those blockages "stones." Your stones have been the wounds keeping you in a state of death.

We know the path that Jesus took to His new life. First, He was crucified, then, he was buried, and then, a stone sealed His grave. The Roman government made sure that a very heavy stone was blocking the grave so that no one would steal His body and claim the resurrection. As we know, a heavy stone was no match for the resurrection power of God. The world's system also sets heavy stones on our "graves" to keep us in bondage.

If you have heard and applied the truths we have presented in this book, you are a candidate for the resurrection power of God to remove your stone and bring you into God's designed prosperity for you life.

### The result is prosperity.
3 John 1:2-4 says, "Beloved, I pray that you may prosper in all things and be in health, just as your soul prospers. For I rejoiced greatly when brethren came and testified of the truth *that is* in you, just as you walk in the truth. I have no greater joy than to hear that my children walk in truth."

*John connected prosperity with three things:*
1. The truth being in his disciples.
2. That his disciples also walked, or lived their lives, in the truth.
3. John equated their potential prosperity with the prosperity of their souls. He said "just as," or in the same measure as your soul prospers, so shall your life prosper. Godly prosperity comes through the Cross, through death and resurrection. It is the same for us, as we go through "deaths" on our journey, we can also see the resurrection of those "deaths."

## Chapter 17 – Your Stone Is Rolled Away

**Definition of prosperity.**

*The Greek word for prosper is euodow euodoo {yoo-od-o'-o}:*

*Prosper, have a prosperous journey; to grant a prosperous and expeditious journey, to lead by a direct and easy way; to grant a successful issue, be successful.*

Psalm 35:27 says, "Let them shout for joy and be glad, Who favor my righteous cause; And let them say continually, 'Let the LORD be magnified, Who has pleasure in the prosperity of His servant.'"

*The word prosper in Hebrew means:*

*shalowm {shaw-lome'} or shalom {shaw-lome'} Peace, well, peaceably, welfare, salute, prosperity, safe, health, peaceable, completeness, soundness, welfare, completeness (in number); safety, soundness (in body); welfare, health, quiet, tranquility, contentment; of human relationships; with God especially in covenant relationship.*

**Prosperity as described in the Bible is "the journey."**

In a journey there will be detours, bumps in the road, maybe even running out of gas. A journey is finally defined not by how easy the travel was, but by reaching the end destination.

Our journey through this life with Jesus was defined in the previous chapter about bearing fruit as covered in Mark chapter 4.

It starts with intimacy with God, the seed of the Word is planted in our hearts as God speaks as in Mark 4, then there is the death of the seed, and finally the resurrection which is fruit. Part of our journey is warfare overcoming Satan's effort to stop the fruit.

There are "ends" or rewards of the journey while we are in this body on earth, and there is a final end to our journey here on earth. If we walk with God as we have been discussing in this book, in spite of sufferings and setbacks, there will be rewards while still here on earth, and Jesus promises the eternal reward that we should always keep our eyes on!

## Chapter 17 – Your Stone Is Rolled Away

Revelation 22:12-13,12 says," And behold, I am coming quickly, and My reward is with Me, to give to every one according to his work. 13 I am the Alpha and the Omega, the Beginning and the End, the First and the Last."

**God can trust you with His prosperity when your soul is healed.**
When your will, mind and emotions are becoming conformed to the image of Christ, then God can trust you with His prosperity. Why? Because then He knows that you are able to possess the prosperity, instead of the prosperity possessing you. Prosperity from the world's system can easily keep you from an intimate relationship with God and it will hamper your dependence upon Him. When it is no longer you who lives but Christ living through you, God will prosper you.

*What is godly prosperity?*

God's definition of prosperity is different from the world's definition. God has a funny way of keeping certain secrets to Himself. All I can say is that if you totally give all of your life to Jesus as Lord, with nothing withheld, and live out that life in the best obedience that you are capable of, that He will bring His definition of prosperity to you that will absolutely confound you. Ephesians 3:20 says, "Now to Him who is able to do exceedingly abundantly above all that we ask or think, according to the power that works in us."

I believe that so many Christians have grossly misunderstood prosperity. I believe that there have been radical excesses in two different directions. Some people say that God wants us to be healthy, wealthy, and not go through sufferings. When I first met the Lord in 1979 I believed that. They attempt to define God's brand of prosperity by the worldly definition of prosperity. Others say that God wants to keep us humble by keeping us poor. Both excesses are wrong. God desires Kingdom of God prosperity for us. Kingdom prosperity is very different, and sometimes its explanation escapes human reason.

I believe that poverty is not supposed to be our end, rather it is to be our entrance into prosperity, a kind of a door through which we walk. Prosperity without death and resurrection will drive a person from God.

**Some aspects of godly prosperity.**
**Fruit of the Spirit.**

I believe that Kingdom prosperity includes first the manifestation of the fruit of the Spirit. Galatians 5:22-23 says, "But the fruit of the Spirit is love, joy, peace, longsuffering, kindness, goodness, faithfulness, gentleness, self-control. Against such there is no law."

**Provisions.**

Next I believe that it includes God's provisions for your earthly life, including, but not limited to, finances, God's choice of a vocation for your life, healthy relationships and other issues dealing with our earthly life. I also believe it includes more than enough for us to survive on so that we may be givers. We are to give to the poor, to ministries and churches that establish God's covenant, and to help Israel in some way.

Deuteronomy 8:18 says, "And you shall remember the LORD your God, for *it is* He who gives you power to get wealth, that He may establish His covenant which He swore to your fathers, as *it is* this day."

I want to make it clear, that when I refer to finances and provisions, that there is no set standard that I am making. Financial prosperity for people in some nations may simply mean having a small garden with vegetables that they may eat and perhaps use some to sell, and use some to feed the poor. This is prosperity for many. For others it may mean being able to operate a good church with a powerful ministry, where the pastor and his family are cared for. For others, God may wish to funnel large sums of money through them for larger projects for the Kingdom of God. We are not to compare ourselves to others.

Nor are we to become discouraged if we have not yet realized financial prosperity. The major issue is to focus on the prosperity of your soul, by, like John said in 3 John, allowing the truth to be in you, and also walking in the truth. Allow God to heal your will, mind and emotions as we have been discussing in the book. Give Him time. Do not become impatient. Do not focus on financial prosperity, but rather focus on your relationship with Him and your walk with Him. Remember, I believe that godly prosperity comes through the doorway of "poverty." When I say poverty, I mean any kind of deprivation, lack or great need.

For those of you in non-Western nations who are experiencing lack of provisions due to a poor economic or political climate I have some advice. Do not look for nor depend upon a Western Christian from a more prosperous nation to support you. That is idolatry. Look upon God for your prosperity: He will provide what you need. Remember, Godly prosperity is not like the world's. God's prosperity comes through death and resurrection on our journey in life.

*Glorifying God.*

And finally, I believe that prosperity includes being used by God to further His Kingdom in our realm of influence. To glorify means to uncover the secret. That could be as a mother raising children, or ministry in our workplaces, and many other types of vocations including church and missionary work.

**Prosperity does not mean the absence of suffering or trials and challenges.**

There are so many different types of prosperity God has for different people. Believers in the persecuted church have to live with a different definition of prosperity. I have visited with Chinese believers who would tell you that they are prospering in prison camps with little food, because they see the Kingdom of God being expanded through their suffering. The church in many persecuted nations is growing in exponential numbers.

Believers who have believed for a physical healing and have not seen the manifestation of it yet, should continue to seek God, but at the same time, should not at all feel condemned or inferior because they do not see their healing. God deals with individuals in many different ways.

## Chapter 17 – Your Stone Is Rolled Away

**The rolling away of the stone relates to resurrection.**
Jesus traded places with you on the Cross. You did not have to suffer the penalty for sin. However, He identified with and included you in the resurrection. When your stone is rolled away, you participate in the resurrection fruit with the Lord.

Look at these examples written in Isaiah showing how prosperity is the fruit that rises from poverty.

**Isaiah 35:1-10 says,**

*1 The wilderness and the wasteland shall be glad for them, And the desert shall rejoice and blossom as the rose;*

*2 It shall blossom abundantly and rejoice, Even with joy and singing. The glory of Lebanon shall be given to it, The excellence of Carmel and Sharon. They shall see the glory of the LORD, The excellency of our God.*

*3 Strengthen the weak hands, And make firm the feeble knees.*

*4 Say to those who are fearful-hearted, "Be strong, do not fear! Behold, your God will come with vengeance, With the recompense of God; He will come and save you."*

*5 Then the eyes of the blind shall be opened, And the ears of the deaf shall be unstopped.*

*6 Then the lame shall leap like a deer, And the tongue of the dumb sing. For waters shall burst forth in the wilderness, And streams in the desert.*

*7 The parched ground shall become a pool, And the thirsty land springs of water; In the habitation of jackals, where each lay, There shall be grass with reeds and rushes.*

*8 A highway shall be there, and a road, And it shall be called the Highway of Holiness. The unclean shall not pass over it, But it shall be for others. Whoever walks the road, although a fool, Shall not go astray.*

*9 No lion shall be there, Nor shall any ravenous beast go up on it; It shall not be found there. But the redeemed shall walk there,*

## Chapter 17 – Your Stone Is Rolled Away

*10 And the ransomed of the LORD shall return, And come to Zion with singing, With everlasting joy on their heads. They shall obtain joy and gladness, And sorrow and sighing shall flee away."*

Isaiah 61 was the prophecy of Jesus' mission statement. It begins with dealing with the poor and downtrodden, the opening of prisons and releasing of captives. It goes on to talk of Satan's demise and the spiritual prosperity of God's redeemed. Then it talks of Jesus overcoming generational curses. It speaks of financial prosperity, and finally, about God's redeemed people serving Him as New Testament priests, or ministers.

**Isaiah 61:1-11 says,**

*1 The Spirit of the Lord GOD is upon Me, Because the LORD has anointed Me To preach good tidings to the poor; He has sent Me to heal the brokenhearted, To proclaim liberty to the captives, And the opening of the prison to those who are bound;*

*2 To proclaim the acceptable year of the LORD, And the day of vengeance of our God; To comfort all who mourn,*

*3 To console those who mourn in Zion, To give them beauty for ashes, The oil of joy for mourning, The garment of praise for the spirit of heaviness; That they may be called trees of righteousness, The planting of the LORD, that He may be glorified."*

*4 And they shall rebuild the old ruins, They shall raise up the former desolations, And they shall repair the ruined cities, The desolations of many generations.*

*5 Strangers shall stand and feed your flocks, And the sons of the foreigner Shall be your plowmen and your vinedressers.*

*6 But you shall be named the priests of the LORD, They shall call you the servants of our God. You shall eat the riches of the Gentiles, And in their glory you shall boast.*

*7 Instead of your shame you shall have double honor, And instead of confusion they shall rejoice in their portion. Therefore in their land they shall possess double; Everlasting joy shall be theirs.*
*8 "For I, the LORD, love justice; I hate robbery for burnt offering; I will direct their work in truth, And will make with them an everlasting covenant.*
*9 Their descendants shall be known among the Gentiles, And their offspring among the people. All who see them shall acknowledge them, That they are the posterity whom the LORD has blessed."*
*10 I will greatly rejoice in the LORD, My soul shall be joyful in my God; For He has clothed me with the garments of salvation, He has covered me with the robe of righteousness, As a bridegroom decks himself with ornaments, And as a bride adorns herself with her jewels.*
*11 For as the earth brings forth its bud, As the garden causes the things that are sown in it to spring forth, So the Lord GOD will cause righteousness and praise to spring forth before all the nations."*

**Joy in the morning speaks of resurrection.**
Psalm 30:5 says, "For His anger *is but for* a moment, His favor *is for* life; Weeping may endure for a night, But joy *comes* in the morning."

Godly prosperity, in my opinion, is what glorifies Jesus, or makes Him known.

John 15:8 says, "By this My Father is glorified, that you bear much fruit; so you will be My disciples." Fruit is a product of resurrection, even in the natural sense.

John 12:24 says, "Most assuredly, I say to you, unless a grain of wheat falls into the ground and dies, it remains alone; but if it dies, it produces much grain."

## Chapter 17 – Your Stone Is Rolled Away

**I believe that if we follow the path laid out the by Apostle Paul in Philippians chapter 3, that we will be on God's course towards the prosperity that He wants for us.**

"[For my determined purpose is] that I may know Him [that I may progressively become more deeply and intimately acquainted with Him, perceiving and recognizing and understanding the wonders of His Person more strongly and more clearly], and that I may in that same way come to know the power outflowing from His resurrection [which it exerts over believers], and that I may so share His sufferings as to be continually transformed [in spirit into His likeness even] to His death, [in the hope] That if possible I may attain to the [spiritual and moral] resurrection [that lifts me] out from among the dead [even while in the body].

Not that I have now attained [this ideal], or have already been made perfect, but I press on to lay hold of (grasp) and make my own, that for which Christ Jesus (the Messiah) has laid hold of me and made me His own" (Philippians 3:10-12, Amplified Bible).

**The following is a quote from Pastor Dr. Kirk Walters – Formerly Administrative and Missions Pastor at Mount Paran North Church of God.**

*He wants us to finish the journey well.*

*So many times we focus on the small, minute details for our measurement of prosperity, i.e. the balance in our bank account or the ability to land the big business deal. God is focused on the really big picture of prosperity.*

*The true indicator of our success in life is the status of our soul. John says he prays that we prosper in all things, including health; but he ties those things to the level of prosperity in our soul.*

*Our responsibility is to live and trust in such a way that at the end of our journey, we can sing, "It is well with my soul!"*

*God's responsibility, if we have lived and trusted well, is to look upon us in perfect judgment and declare, "Well done, good and faithful servant. Enter in the joys of the Lord!"*

*That's true prosperity!"*

# Appendix A

## Relationship Skills

**1. 1. Make a firm decision to pursue the relationship.** Offer yourself completely to God. This is our task to complete the mighty blood covenant offered to us by an awesome God. When we were born again our "old self" was crucified and it died. We were given a new nature; we are now new creations, returned to "normal" because now the Mighty God dwells in us. It is Him and Him alone that lives in us! The only remnant of the "old self" is in our thinking process. We have to continually renew our minds to these facts.

As we do, we will not be so aware of the demands of the "old self," which are always selfish. That selfishness causes fear, anger, control over circumstances, and many other horrible feelings.

I like to do this. As my "self" rises up, I say to it, "Get back to the grave, you are dead! I am not going to engage in fear and worry. I am not going to have to be noticed and praised."

***Meditate on these Scriptures.***
**Romans 12:1, 2 says,**

*"1 I beseech you therefore, brethren, by the mercies of God, that you present your bodies a living sacrifice, holy, acceptable to God, which is your reasonable service.*

*2 And do not be conformed to this world, but be transformed by the renewing of your mind, that you may prove what is that good and acceptable and perfect will of God."*

**Galatians 2:20 says,**

*"20 "I have been crucified with Christ; it is no longer I who live, but Christ lives in me; and the life which I now live in the flesh I live by faith in the Son of God, who loved me and gave Himself for me."*

**Romans 6:6 says,**

## Chapter 17 – Your Stone Is Rolled Away

> *"6 knowing this, that our old man was crucified with Him, that the body of sin might be done away with, that we should no longer be slaves of sin."*

**Matthew 6:33 says,**

> *"33 "But seek first the kingdom of God and His righteousness, and all these things shall be added to you."*

**2. Take time to listen: You must take in His Word.** Words are blood covenant containers. The Word of God is Jesus Himself; it is not a book of promises to pick and choose from. The Word of God should be pursued as a regular and daily relationship skill and should be looked at as listening to your Lord, Jesus Himself. Ask Him to speak. The Word is supernatural and it produces faith in the same way natural food produces energy. Jesus said that He is the true manna that gives eternal life. Write down what you feel He is speaking.

**3. Take time to speak: Your words.** Two-way journaling and being gut-level honest is an important way to increase your relationship with God. Write down exactly how you feel. Honesty with your blood covenant partner Jesus will cause your sin to go on Him. You cannot and will not overcome any issue in life without this gut-level honesty. We suggest two-way journaling. This is a great way to allow the "flow" of the Holy Spirit to speak to you personal and intimate things. First, get in a quiet place, set your mind on Jesus, and begin to worship Him. You write down what you want to tell or ask Jesus. Then, write down what you hear in your spirit. At first, there may be some mistakes, but through faith and practice, He will be real to you.

> ***Ways to discern whose voice you are hearing.***
> God's voice: Affirms, corrects, direction (truth).
> Satan's voice: Keeps us bound in failure with lies and condemnation.
> Self's voice, or our flesh: justifies, rationalizes, denies and projects or blames others.
> ***Testing to see if we are hearing God's voice.***

Is it scriptural?
Does it glorify Jesus?
Is there a witness in my spirit?
Does it edify or tear down?
Does it produce freedom or bondage?
*Ways God speaks to us.*
The Bible. Revelation knowledge through the Holy Spirit.
The Body of Christ: Fellow believers, pastors, counselors. Be careful to not depend solely on this.
Quiet time: Holy Spirit's voice. (Psalm 139:23-24, 1 John 1:9).
Circumstances and situations in everyday life (Jeremiah 32:8).
Accountability Partner: Often it is wise to have a trusted friend who will be bold enough to hold you accountable for issues in your life.

**4. Take time to speak: His Words.** The antagonist, Satan, and his assigned demons constantly are on task to come against your effort to relate to Jesus and to overcome. Only you can resist them. Jesus gave you the authority and responsibility to speak His Word against them. God told Joshua in Joshua 1:8, "This Book of the Law shall not depart from your mouth, but you shall meditate in it day and night, that you may observe to do according to all that is written in it. For then you will make your way prosperous, and then you will have good success."

*One idea for doing this is:*
Read Psalms and Proverbs by the day. You should read ALOUD five Psalms every morning. Use the system of the calendar, i.e., on the 3rd of the month read Psalms 3, 33, 63, 93 and 123. Also read Proverb 3. In this system the student will read all Psalms and Proverbs every month. Using this system renews the mind, speaks the Word to Satan, and allows the suffering student to relate his/her emotions to the Psalmist's. Provisions can be made for months with 31 days, and for Psalm 119.

Also be sensitive to the Holy Spirit Who will give you a Word of warfare for a particular situation.

**5. Meditation.** Meditation on the Word is very important and extremely valuable. I quoted Joshua 1:8 above which tells us to meditate day and night. Psalm 1:2-3 says, "But his delight *is* in the law of the LORD, And in His law he meditates day and night. He shall be like a tree Planted by the rivers of water, That brings forth its fruit in its season, Whose leaf also shall not wither; And whatever he does shall prosper."

Meditation on the Word displaces and replaces your carnal thinking which is a major feat. It also allows the Word to get down deep into your heart. The word meditate is related to a cow chewing her cud. She chews it, swallows it, regurgitates it, and then starts the process over again, and again, and again. This will allow the Word to go deeply into your heart, and will give the Holy Spirit an opportunity to speak something personal to you from the Word.

**6. Fasting.** Fasting is an important discipline. There are many types of fasts, and I will not cover that subject here. The main advantage of fasting is that it denies the strongest desire of the flesh, to eat. In doing so one is able to hear the Holy Spirit better. Remember, the flesh lusts against the Spirit and the Spirit against the flesh, Galatians 5:17. I have read that when a person is hungry, even his/her natural hearing is better.

**7. Obey God**. Ask God to give you something simple, something small every day that you may obey. It may be just encouraging another, it may be not driving down the same street that fed your addiction; it may be confessing your sin to Him. It may be taking a thought captive, or forgiving someone, or perhaps giving a financial gift.

*This is a big thing!* John 14:21-23 says that when we obey His Word that He will reveal more and more of Himself to us. Once you have "seen" Jesus, relationship with Him will no longer be a discipline, but it will be a passionate pursuit.

**End Notes**

[1] The Spiritual Man, Watchman Nee author.

2 Many references are made to Dunklin Memorial Church. We have inserted several quotes from their book Inner Healing. We give thanks to that wonderful ministry in Florida USA that has made a valuable contribution to the Body of Christ. Many of their leaders and authors are recovered addicts who now serve the Lord Jesus Christ.
Copyright * 1992 by Dunklin Memorial Church – Used by permission ISOB

**My true identity**
I believe:
That in Christ Jesus all of my sins, past, present and future have been completely forgiven. I have simply received His free gift by faith. There was nothing I could have ever done to earn it. And there is nothing I can ever do to lose it. His amazing love is absolutely unconditional.

In Christ I have been given a brand new identity. No longer am I in Adam. I am a New Creation! Jesus sits at the right hand of the Father constantly interceding for me. He is never ashamed, and even when I fail He lovingly reminds me of whose I really am. The enemy no longer has any power over me because he was once and forever defeated at Calvary. When Satan tries to bring up my past to discourage me I will be prompted to immediately remind him of his future. Greater is the Lord Jesus who lives in me than he who temporarily rules this fallen old world!

In Christ I am no longer a slave to my feelings. The truth about me is what God says REGARDLESS of my emotions. Since I now possess the mind of Christ I am no longer bound up in the lies of Satan. The Holy Spirit readily exposes his tricks. Any and every thought that is presented to me MUST pass through a True/False "filter." If the thought is not pure, holy, and glorifying to my Father, it is clearly from the enemy. In the name of Jesus I will reject his ungodly thoughts and he must flee!

In Christ Jesus I have been raised to walk in newness of life. Abundant Life, Eternal Life, His Life! In fact, I have already been made a citizen of Heaven! What joy fills my soul! Since my Father is always for me, who would dare come against me? I am more than a conqueror. The victory is already mine!

In Christ there is eternal hope. Worry and fear are no longer my constant companions. Since they are lies from Satan they are inconsistent with my true identity. I am now alive to Truth and dead to sin. Jesus is my all in all. He is everything to me. I will not worship any other person or thing. There is no one above Him. He is all I really need. He is my Way, my Truth, and my Life. He is enough.

-Anonymous

**Closing prayer for you.**
Ephesians 3:16-21 says "that He would grant you, according to the riches of His glory, to be strengthened with might through His Spirit in the inner man, that Christ may dwell in your hearts through faith; that you, being rooted and grounded in love, may be able to comprehend with all the saints what *is* the width and length and depth and height-- to know the love of Christ which passes knowledge; that you may be filled with all the fullness of God. Now to Him who is able to do exceedingly abundantly above all that we ask or think, according to the power that works in us, to Him *be* glory in the church by Christ Jesus to all generations, forever and ever. Amen."

www.ingramcontent.com/pod-product-compliance
Lightning Source LLC
Chambersburg PA
CBHW061639040426
42446CB00010B/1492